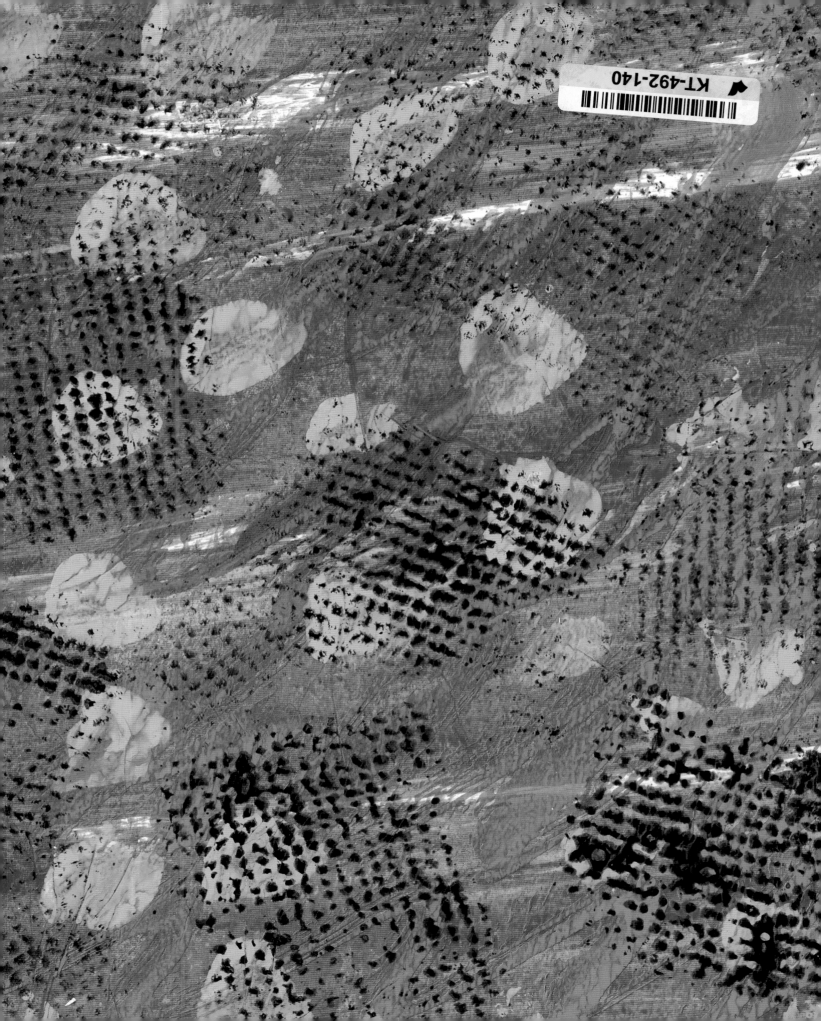

THE ART OF ERIC CARLE

THE ART OF ERIC CARLE

PHILOMEL BOOKS · NEW YORK

The Children's Literature Center in the Library of Congress, a respected place of study and research, has celebrated and supported authors and artists of children's books since its inception in 1963.
The idea for this retrospective on Eric Carle's life and work originated at one of the Center's annual International Children's Book Days.
Special thanks and deep appreciation go to Dr. Sybille A. Jagusch, the Chief of the Children's Literature Center, for her support and cooperation.

Library of Congress Cataloging-in-Publication Data
Carle, Eric.
The art of Eric Carle / Eric Carle.   p.   cm.
"Books by Eric Carle" : p. Includes index.
1. Carle, Eric—Themes, motives. 2. Picture books for children — United States.
I. Title. N6537.C3443A4 1996 741.6'42'092—dc20 95-24940 CIP

ISBN: 0-399-22937-X
10 9 8 7 6 5 4 3 2

Many thanks to friends and family who provided photographs from their collections.

Photograph of Stuttgart on page 23 from Die Zerstörung: Stuttgart 1944 und danach, by Hannes Kilian published by Quadriga Publishing Company; copyright © 1984 by Hannes Kilian. Reproduced with the permission of the photographer.

Thanks to Stephen Petegorsky Photgraphy for providing photographic services.

The demonstration photographs in the chapter How Eric Carle Creates His Art and the photograph of Bill Martin Jr and Eric Carle on page 35 were taken by Sigrid Estrada.

Photograph on page 37 was taken by Marie Frank.

Photograph on page 47 was taken by Wolfgang Dietrich.

Photograph of Eric Carle in his studio on page 71 and those photographs on pages 66, 67 and 38 were taken by Motoko Inoue.

Book design by Eric Carle and Motoko Inoue.

The text is set in Walbaum Regular and Italic, Lithos Bold, and Gil Sans Light and Italic.

Grateful acknowledgment is given here for the permissions to reprint the images from Eric Carle's books published by the following publishers.

Dowaya
All in a Day projected by Mitsumasa Anno/JFC Copyright © 1986 by Kûsô Kôbô/JFC and Eric Carle. Original Japanese edition published in 1986 by Dowaya, Tokyo, under the title ALL IN A DAY.

Farrar, Straus & Giroux
Why Noah Chose the Dove by Isaac Bashevis Singer. Copyright © 1973 by Isaac Bashevis Singer; Pictures opyright © 1974 by Eric Carle

HarperCollins Publishers
Do You Want to Be My Friend? Copyright © 1976 by Eric Carle
The Secret Birthday Message Copyright © 1971 by Eric Carle
The Mixed-Up Chameleon Copyright © 1975, 1984 by Eric Carle
The Grouchy Ladybug Copyright © 1977 by Eric Carle

Henry Holt and Company, Inc.
Brown Bear, Brown Bear, What Do You See? by Bill Martin Jr. Pictures by Eric Carle. Copyright © 1967, 1983 by Holt, Rinehart and Winston, Inc.
Polar Bear, Polar Bear, What Do You Hear? by Bill Martin Jr. Illustrations by Eric Carle. Text copyright © 1991 by Bill Martin Jr. Illustrations copyright © 1991 by Eric Carle.

Orchard Books
The Lamb and the Butterfly by Arnold Sundgaard, illustration by Eric Carle. Illustration copyright © 1988 by Eric Carle.
Eric Carle's Treasury of Classic Stories for Children by Aesop, Hans Christian Andersen and the Brothers Grimm, selected, retold and illustrated by Eric Carle. Special content of this volume copyright © 1988 by Eric Carle Corp. Text and illustration copyright © 1976, 1978, 1980 and 1988 by Eric Carle.

Philomel Books
1,2,3 to the Zoo Copyright © 1968 by Eric Carle
The Very Hungry Caterpillar Copyright © 1969 and 1987 by Eric Carle
The Honeybee and the Robber Copyright © 1981 by Eric Carle
The Very Busy Spider Copyright © 1984 by Eric Carle Corp.
Animals Animals compiled by Laura Whipple, Illustration copyright © 1989 by Eric Carle
The Very Quiet Cricket Copyright © 1990 by Eric Carle Corp.
Dragons Dragons compiled by Laura Whipple, Compilation copyright © 1991 by Philomel Books; Illustration copyright © 1991 by Eric Carle Corp.
Draw Me a Star Copyright © 1992 by Eric Carle
Today is Monday Copyright © 1993 by Eric Carle
My Apron Copyright © 1994 by Eric Carle
The Very Lonely Firefly Copyright © 1995 by Eric Carle
Little Cloud Copyright © 1996 by Eric Carle

Simon & Schuster Books for Young Readers
Pancakes, Pancakes! by Eric Carle. Copyright © 1990 Eric Carle Corp.
The Tiny Seed by Eric Carle. Copyright © 1987 Eric Carle Corp.
Rooster's Off to See the World by Eric Carle. Copyright © 1972 Eric Carle Corp.
Walter the Baker by Eric Carle. Copyright © 1972, 1995 Eric Carle.
Have You Seen My Cat? by Eric Carle. Copyright © 1987 Eric Carle Corp.
The Foolish Tortoise/The Greedy Python by Richard Buckley, illustrated by Eric Carle. Illustration copyright © 1985 Eric Carle.
The Mountain That Loved a Bird by Alice McLerran, illustrated by Eric Carle. Illustration copyright © 1985 Neugebauer Press USA Inc.
Papa, Please Get the Moon for Me by Eric Carle. Copyright © 1986 Eric Carle Corp.
A House for Hermit Crab by Eric Carle. Copyright © 1987 Eric Carle Corp.

I See a Song Copyright © 1973 by Eric Carle. Originally published by Thomas Y. Crowell Company. Reissued in 1995 as paperback edition by Scholastic Inc.
Chip Has Many Brothers by Hans Baumann. Originally published by Gerstenberg Verlag under the title Tschip hat viele Brüder. Text copyright © 1983 Gerstenberg Verlag. Illustration copyright © 1983 by Eric Carle. Reissued in 1995 as paperback edition by Scholastic Inc. under the title Thank You Brother Bear.

CONTENTS

Leonard S. Marcus
INTRODUCTION

When the 23-year-old graphic designer Eric Carle returned from Germany in the spring of 1952 to live permanently in the United States, New York was the dazzling new world capital of the visual arts. In the decades before World War II, Europe had stood at the forefront of innovation in graphic art and design. After the war, however, the epicenter of visual communication shifted to the west, and buoyant, often irreverent fresh approaches to advertising art, the poster, the illustrated magazine, and the children's picture book blossomed and cross-pollinated. It was in this intensely fertile creative environment that the American-born, German-educated Carle immersed himself, and emerged first as an accomplished commercial artist and then, by a metamorphosis not unlike his well-known caterpillar's, as the maker of children's books of radiant tenderness, poetic insight, and rare graphic distinction.

Mr. Leonard S. Marcus is one of the children's book world's foremost critics and historians. He is the author of Margaret Wise Brown: Awakened by the Moon *and is chief children's book reviewer at* Parenting *magazine.*

As a storyteller, Carle aligned himself early on with the age-old tradition of the fable, a deceptively simple narrative genre that bears a striking resemblance to contemporary graphics in its search for irreducibly clear, instantly recognizable images and symbols. As Carle's hungry caterpillar, mixed-up chameleon, busy spider, and lonely firefly wiggle or wing their way toward their moment of self-discovery, the reader easily finds his or her own point of identification with the tale.

The bugs and beasts one meets in traditional fables like Aesop's are essentially humans in animal dress: the focus remains firmly fixed on human nature. In contrast, Carle's tales convey a genuine interest in all of nature, from the smallest (and peskiest) insect to the life-giving sun. The world presents itself in the stories as both a beguilingly vast and various place and a fundamentally safe and

Caterpillar eating his way through plums

Firefly with his friends

Chameleon being himself

hospitable home ground. While reassuring the young that the world does indeed care about them, Carle also shows (just as importantly for children's growth) that much lies beyond the self, and the human realm, to know and explore.

There is much within Carle's books that does not have to be expressed in words because it can be seen—or just imagined. The airy white space that forms one of the signature elements of his art does not simply create contrast for the bold colors it surrounds: it leaves breathing room for the child's own daydreams. Likewise, Carle's preference for collage (a technique favored by postwar graphic artists in their quest for a more free-spirited language of visual expression) is a preference for a type of picture-making with which the young themselves have already had some experience. Carle's gentle, incisive illustrations are an open invitation to

readers to make more pictures of their own, and to regard his books not only as finished works but as challenging, playful points of departure.

It is an invitation that children throughout the world have taken to heart.

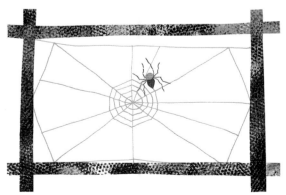

Busy spider weaving her web

Left: *Karl and Anna Oelschläger, my maternal grandparents*
Right: *Sophie and Gustav Carle, my paternal grandparents*

Left: *Johanna, my mother*
Right: *Erich, my father*

Me at six months

AUTOBIOGRAPHY
A life in words and pictures

y father, who had a way with pencil and brush, wanted to become an artist, but his father, a customs official in Stuttgart, Germany, decreed otherwise. A civil service job would be much more respected, and one should not overlook the benefits that the state bestowed upon its faithful servants. A large *Ehrenurkunde,* a certificate for honorable services rendered, signed with big blue letters by Chancellor von Hindenburg, graced the wall above an ornate chest in my grandparents' living room. The *Ehrenurkunde,* and a golden pocket watch, which my grandfather every so often pompously withdrew from his vest, attested to the validity of his philosophy.

And so my unenthusiastic father was apprenticed to a small town *Bürgermeister* to learn the ways of city government. But no great love was lost between my father and the town management, and in 1925 he decided to leave. Like so many others at that time, he emigrated to America. He was twenty-one years old when he and his sixteen-year-old sister arrived in the United States. Soon he would also sponsor his younger brother. He found a job with the Easy Washer Company in Syracuse, New York. For the next ten years, he cheerfully spray-painted washing machines "making a steady forty dollars a week, even during the Depression," as he often repeated throughout his life, which convinced me that forty dollars was a considerable amount of money.

Before my father left Germany, he had fallen in love with Johanna Oelschläger, a tall, pretty girl of seventeen with blonde hair and blue eyes. Now letters began to flow back and forth between them. One of my father's letters that has survived shows a pencil drawing of Rudolph Valentino in a desert tent surrounded by palm trees. In 1927, Johanna, now nineteen years old and unable to resist the charm and draftsmanship of these letters, left for the New World. My father met her at the New York harbor and from there a train rushed them to upstate New York. My mother, who spoke no English, found a job as a maid with a kind, wealthy family. Soon her sisters and brothers back in Germany began to wear the wealthy family's hand-me-down sweaters, shoes, and knickerbockers. I understand that the knickerbockers especially were quite a hit.

In 1928 my parents were married in the German

Lutheran Church in Syracuse. I was born in 1929, "thirteen months after the wedding," as my mother told everyone until her death.

I have the persistent impression that my young parents were happy and content with their life. They had a small circle of friends, mostly other German emigrants. Like most Germans, my parents worshiped nature, and with their friends they enjoyed camping, swimming, and boating in the nearby Finger Lakes. Many weekends were spent among the trees and lakes at the nature camp. Fading photographs show them and their friends with open smiles. I do not always seem to share their sense of joy—or is it the glaring sun that makes me squint my eyes and furrow my brow?

Even as a small child, I was curious about animals, especially small ones, and I remember the excitement of lifting stones or peeling back the bark of dead trees to discover the living things that crawled, crept, and scurried about there. This love of and curiosity about ants, beetles, salamanders, and worms had been awakened in me by my father. He'd take me on

walks through meadows and woods, and explain, as we explored, the often peculiar life cycles of these small creatures, which we had discovered underneath a rock or dead leaf. Afterward, he carefully put these little animals back into their original places and covered them up again.

One day, as I was by myself, I discovered a snake sunning itself. Slowly, carefully, I put my small hands around it and was immediately enthralled by its smooth, clean skin as its gentle movements tingled against my palms. Then I rushed with the snake in my hands toward a group of grown-ups who sat around a campfire, to show off my trophy. Panic! Screams! I was puzzled. I had expected "Ohhs" and "Ahhs." Only my father, who had been with the group, remained calm and reassured the others, now hiding behind trees, that what we had here was a perfectly harmless garter snake.

In 1935 I started school in Syracuse. I remember vividly a sun-filled room, large sheets of paper, colorful paints, and fat brushes. One day my mother was asked to see the teacher. Convinced that her son had misbehaved—why else would a parent be asked to come to the school?—she was immensely relieved to be told that her boy not only enjoyed drawing and painting but that he was good at it. It was impressed upon my mother that from now on she was to encourage and nurture this talent. This was advice she would honor for the rest of her life.

My mother, more Teutonic by nature than my father, believed above all that children must obey the wishes and demands of their parents. "A child must be broken before he is six years

And, indeed, my ears did stick out! 1934

old," I once overheard her telling another mother. "After that it is too late." But when I reached for my pencils, crayons, watercolors, and paper, she became strangely unsure of herself; partly awed, partly confused, she left me alone to enjoy the world of lines and colors.

My father had a somewhat Gallic disposition. His forefathers, with compatriots, had left France many generations before during one of the many religious confrontations in the Middle Ages, to settle in southwest Germany. This group remained French, living closely together in several small villages until the turn of this century, when they began to marry "outside."

In 1934 my Carle grandmother came to America to visit us. *"Du hast Schlappohren,"* she told me

With my father on the ship to Germany

as I sat in her lap. And, indeed, my ears did stick out! I spoke only English but understood German. We smiled and chuckled together. She had come to see her children; three of her five children now lived in the United States. Now she implored them to come back to Germany. *"Alles is gut,"* she told them, "Everything is good." She promised gifts and she told them about the rising leader, Adolf Hitler, and claimed that he had eliminated unemployment, inflation, and hunger. Her own children ignored her pleas, but in my mother the seed of homesickness had been planted. Soon we began to pack things. I packed my *Mickey Mouse* and *Flash Gordon* comic books, a little leather cap that had WANNA BUY A DUCK? written on it, a tomahawk that my father had carved for me, and a picture of George Washington printed in garish colors on a two-by-three-inch piece of plywood. Several scratches marred his face, which must have been the reason why someone had thrown it into a garbage can from where I had retrieved it. The comic books, the funny cap, and the toma-hawk are all gone, but George Washington, now somewhat pale, is still with me and on display in my home. I am not certain what this little

print meant to me then or why I still treasure it.

Across from us in Syracuse lived an Italian family. One of the children, a girl my age, led me down to the cool basement of their house, where her family had withdrawn to escape the summer heat. Her old grandmother handed me a warm loaf of bread. It was my farewell gift.

The next day our journey to Germany began. I was six years old.

For a short time, we lived next door to my mother's parents in an apartment on the third floor on *Eichstrasse* in Stuttgart. But soon we moved to *Dieterlestrasse*, where my Oelschläger grandfather had bought a four-story house; each floor had two bedrooms, a living room, and a kitchen. It took my grandfather no time at all to fill up his house with members of his family.

As a cowboy in America, 1934

In a Tyrolean outfit in Germany, 1935

On the top floor lived my Uncle Gustav, his wife, and their child. Gustav's mother-in-law, *Frau Erdmann*, a World War I widow, often visited for long periods of time. On the third floor lived my grandparents, Karl and Anna, and their daughter Helene. Helene married relatively late in her life, and during World War II, her husband, Ernst, moved into her small room with her. Ernst, however, was soon drafted into the *Wehrmacht*, the German army, and lost his life in Russia when Lore, his daughter, was still a baby. We lived on the floor below them. On the ground floor lived a family of four not related to any of us. When they moved out later, Rudolf, my mother's younger brother, his wife, their child, and his mother-in-law, also a World War I widow, moved in.

It didn't take long for family fights to break out. In all fairness, though, it must be said that these quarrels were often interrupted, either because the bickering had grown too tiresome or a truce had somehow been instigated. During family gatherings, weddings, birthdays, baptisms, or anniversaries, my father spoke glowingly about America. But if he didn't, a relative was sure to shout, "Erich, tell us about *Amerika!*" Then he became animated, and his stories became more and more embellished.

My new playmates at first called me *Amerikaner*, which was then shortened to *Ami*. Later I was called *Amerzke*, which changed to *Setzke*. Even today, my former German school friends call me *Setzke*. I roamed the backyards and climbed fences and, from a distance, fell in love with Ursula, a neighborhood girl of five who reminded me both of my Italian girlfriend and of Shirley Temple. (Twelve years later, I dared

With my first grade class, Stuttgart, 1936

to invite Ursula to a dance!) At many a *Familie Fest* I was asked to sing Shirley Temple's song, *On the Good Ship Lollipop.* Many people in town had relatives in the United States or had lived there themselves, so I was easily accepted by everyone. In fact, being an American made me somewhat special to my playmates .

Before long, I had forgotten English and spoke only German. In 1936, I was sent to school to begin the second round of my education. I remember this vividly, too—a small room with narrow windows, a hard pencil, a small sheet of paper, and a stern warning not to make mistakes. Three days later, I was the first of my class to be introduced to an old German tradition: corporal punishment. For a minor infraction, I received "three on each hand." That meant that I bravely stepped up to my teacher and stuck out one little hand, palm upward. Three times the teacher, armed with a thin bamboo stick, struck my outstretched hand with all his might. Then I held out my other hand for a repeat performance. Then, still bravely, I returned to my seat and held back my tears while three painful welts erupted on each of my palms. That evening, I asked my parents to write a note to the teacher.

"Tell him," I said, "that your son is not suited for an education." Certainly not an unreasonable conclusion at that stage of my young life. Finally, my mother sat down and wrote the desired note to my teacher, the letter that would solve all my problems. Now I would simply have no more school. I don't know what my mother put into that letter. But to this day, I have not forgotten my teacher's wrath when I returned to school—and, of course, I returned. He grew taller, he turned purple, he screamed, he fumed and foamed, he thoroughly humiliated me. I felt physically and emotionally devastated. There was no way out after all. Obviously, my German teacher had detected a certain undesirable freedom of behavior in this little American boy, something that did not conform to the local norm. The boy had to be broken in. This was his duty, a duty he could not shirk. He had simply waited for the earliest possible moment to strike, to do what was his responsibility. Only one thing was left to me, and I did it for the next ten years: I hated school! But outwardly I did not show it. Indeed, my first report card states: "Eric is a friendly and obedient child. However, he should learn to participate more." It seems that I had learned my lesson well!

But almost daily I asked my parents, "When are we going home?" When I realized that we were not going to return to America, I decided that I would become a bridge builder, build a bridge from Stuttgart to Syracuse, and take my beloved Oelschläger *Oma*, my grandmother, by her hand and lead her across the wide ocean.

My boyhood friend in Syracuse wrote to me in awkward letters:

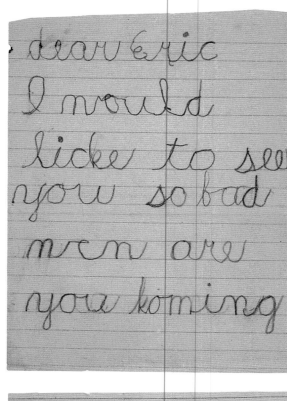

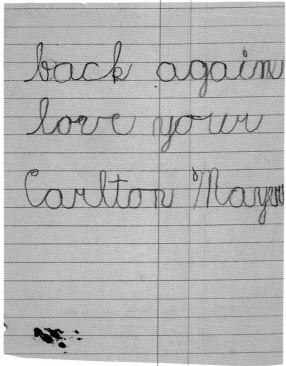

Twenty years later, I went to his door, unannounced, and asked him, "Do you know me?" Without a moment's hesitation, he answered, "You're Eric!" Now, more than fifty years later, I still have his precious letter. In my heart, I have dedicated my book *Do You Want to Be My Friend?* to this first and deeply felt friendship.

All these events, and feelings about them, have made a lasting impression on me. The memories of the following years seem less continuous, more scattered into clusters of time, and often I find it hard to establish their chronological order.

At the end of the school year in Germany, just before the long summer vacation, all schoolchildren underwent a simple medical examination. Its main purpose was to establish one's weight. I had been a finicky eater and was considered underweight. A fat child was

someone parents were proud of. "Eat! Eat! It's good for you!" was the battle cry of every mother. It caused my mother endless pain that I did not finish my plate, picked at the vegetables, or simply refused to eat. Annual medical examinations changed all that. Children under a certain weight, like myself, were sent to an *Erholungsheim,* or recreation home. This *Erholungsheim* had very little to do with recreation. Kindly but resolute ladies, whom we were told to call *Tante,* aunt, made sure that the children ate a lot, took their cod liver oil regularly, and rested for hours each day. We also marched in circles in a steamy room, inhaling saline vapors, which were supposed to be good for one's lungs. Each *Tante* was totally dedicated to the principle that her charge would leave the *Erholungsheim* many pounds heavier, even if it meant placing a helpless child on her lap and forcibly stuffing lumpy semolina pudding down his or her throat. Throwing up made no impression whatsoever; the mess was quietly cleaned up, and the stuffing continued. That way, I gained four pounds in three weeks. Of course, I lost these pounds as soon as I returned home.

After another stay at the *Erholungsheim* the following year, I made the connection between the medical examination and the trip to the *Erholungsheim* and managed thereafter to pass the required minimum weight limit.

Now followed several summer vacations on farms owned by distant relatives or friends of my grandmother. I loved the smell of the stables and being near the sturdy workhorses, grazing cows, clucking chickens, and grunting pigs. I learned to milk a cow, although I must admit that my little city hands got tired awfully fast. I watched the bees for hours as they flew to and from their hive. I searched for eggs hidden among the piles of straw in the barn. I learned to wield a scythe; to turn hay so that it dried properly; to harness a horse or an ox; to find *Preiselbeeren,* cranberries, in a nearby bog, *Heidelbeeren,* blueberries, at the edge of the woods, and mushrooms on the forest floor. No one needed to urge me to eat now. With hearty appetite, I ate slices of crisp-crusted dark bread spread with lard that had been rendered with pieces of apple and onion, and drank fresh buttermilk, which had been chilled in a big crock on the cold cellar steps. On holidays and Sundays there was onion pie made with thick cream and sliced onions, or *Apfelkuchen mit Brösel,* apple tart with sweet bread crumbs. I remember resting in the shade of an enormous oak tree, surrounded by shimmering yellow fields, listening to crickets.

My Oelschläger *Oma* had told me that she was one of ten children, one boy and nine girls. I vividly recall five of her sisters but not the others; perhaps they had died young. And although her only brother lived in the same city, I never met him. The sisters often spoke of him affection-ately. Toward the end of World War II he was killed near his home in a low-level attack by an Allied fighter plane. Some of my *Oma*'s sisters lived in Stuttgart, and others nearby, and visits and countervisits were common. And even though none of them had a telephone, my grandmother had a sure instinct for a pending visit. Then she began to bake *Gugelhupf* and *Hefenkrantz,* and if that didn't seem adequate, she'd send me to the *Konditorei,* bakery, for some *Schokolade Torte.* The "good" silver and china were polished, the furniture dusted, and the "good" room aired. Finally, the coffee was ground and the kettle put on the unlit stove. Invariably, she was right. The doorbell rang, and the stove was lit to boil the water.

All my aunts (great-aunts, really) loved me, pulled me to their ample bosoms, and kissed me generously. Soon they'd open their handbags, rummage among their handkerchiefs, combs, small bottles of perfume, fountain pens, and other paraphernalia to discover that they had a gift for me: a few coins, a piece of candy, or some chocolate. When the afternoon *Kaffeeklatsch* had stretched into the evening, I was sent across the street to the restaurant *Linde* with a pitcher to fetch a liter of beer. "But make sure that they don't give you too much foam," I was cautioned. All my aunts had a habit of politely refusing food and drink; then my grandmother, with even greater politeness, would insist on filling their plates and glasses. It was all an accepted ritual with a foregone conclusion. It is with great fondness that I recall these visits.

One of my aunts, *Tante* Mina, was special to me,

My beloved Oelschläger Oma

or was it really her husband, *Onkel* August? August liked parties, wine, and a good story, preferably his own, told by himself. Best of all, he was a painter. Every so often I was invited to spend a weekend with my *Tante* Mina and *Onkel* August. I'd take the trolley number sixteen to the *Schlossplatz,* get off and cross the *Marktplatz,* passing the *Schillerkirche* first, until I came to their house, an old, crooked-timbered building in the oldest part of the city. After I had rung the bell, I'd sense that I was being observed through a small round mirror fastened to their window on an upper floor. Attached to a rope, a small basket was lowered to me; inside, under a cloth, was a large, ornate key to let myself in. As I climbed the dark and winding stairs, I would inhale the different smells on each landing until I sniffed oil paints, linseed oil, and turpentine. At the door my aunt would hug and kiss me, and push me into their kitchen to stuff me with goodies, fearing that I was near starvation from the forty-five minute trolley car ride. (You see, all the foods in my book *The Very Hungry Caterpillar* are not just figments of my imagination!) Then I would go into my uncle's studio, a small unused bedroom, and sit down next to him. I would find him carefully applying layers of oil paint from his palette to the canvas, which might show a snow-capped mountain, a lake, some birch and pine trees, a chalet, and colorful pieces of clothing strung from the chalet's balcony for drying. Finally he would turned toward me, his mischievous eyes peering over the rims of his glasses, as he had done many times before.

"*Onkel,* tell me a story!"

"First you have to wind up my thinking machine," he replied. Putting my hand near his temple, I began to crank an imaginary lever.

"Halt! I have a story for you!"

How well I remember those blissful moments when he'd tell me a story: "Have I told you about the time when I was a collier in the hot belly of a freighter to Hoboken and how I worked there in a sauerkraut factory while the ship was being unloaded?"

"No," I lied.

"Or the time when my friend Buckel and I converted to Catholicism?"

"No," I lied again. How could anyone ever get enough of his stories? How Buckel and August, both Catholics, born to Catholic parents, and raised as Catholics, still managed to become converted to Catholicism was actually my favorite of all.

Later, when the war broke out, Mina and August's only son, their pride and joy, Rolf, volunteered and joined the German Army. He was killed in Russia, outside Moscow. After that, *Onkel* August's thinking machine refused to be wound up.

On my way to school I often passed a small department store on the *Adolf Hitler Strasse.* Occasionally I had bought a toy there for myself, or some thread or canning jars for my mother. But one day as I passed, clothing, furniture, hardware, toys, and much more lay strewn and torn beyond the shattered windows. A large Star of David had been painted roughly across

a broken door that was off its hinges. The damaged building was cordoned off, and a policeman ordered me to move on, to be on my way to school. This was the *Kristallnacht*, the Night of Broken Glass, 1938, when open anti-Semitism erupted in Nazi Germany.

Summer, 1939. My father has put enough money aside for us to afford our first family vacation. We stay at a small *pension* in Berneck in the Black Forest. My mother looks radiant, my father handsome, and I feel thoroughly blessed to have my parents all to myself. I am reminded of the old days at nature camp in Syracuse. My father and I rename the local pond "Lake Wakamba." We rent an old rowboat with peeling paint and pretend that it is a birchbark canoe and we are Indians in feathered headdresses as we glide along the glassy surface, howling bloodcurdling war cries at the non-Indians in their Sunday best strolling along the shores. But soon, even in our little paradise, there is talk about a real war. Newspaper headlines mention England's Neville Chamberlain, the *Maginot* Line in France, and Poland's hostility toward Germany. We leave Berneck sooner than we had planned.

September, 1939. Hitler's mesmerizing voice shouts from our *Volksempfänger*, people's radio:

"…our troops are shooting back!" His army, the *Wehrmacht*, attacks Poland. World War II has begun. My father is drafted that very same day.

Blitzkrieg. Poland is overrun by the Nazis in a few weeks; so, a little later, is France. Denmark, Norway, Holland, and Belgium are taken within days. Homecoming German soldiers, victorious, tan, and smiling, march through the streets, waving from trucks and tanks as flowers are tossed at them by cheering masses.

Then comes the startling invasion into the Soviet Union, breaking the German-Soviet pact of alliance. The Balkan countries are overrun. The *Swastika* flag flutters above the Acropolis in Greece. Hitler seems invincible. He declares war on the United States. The U-boat wolf packs sink ship after ship.

Like all his German-born schoolmates, the little American boy is swept up in the mounting tide of patriotism and Nazi propaganda. My schoolmates and I request autographs from our heroes, General Rommel, General Jodl, and others. Daily, the people's radio blares forth accounts of Hitler's latest victories, and people respond.

"Sieg Heil! Sieg Heil!"

But after a while, the victory announcements become less frequent. The U-boats sink fewer and fewer enemy ships. The *Wehrmacht* in Russia retreats. "Strategic retreats. Shortening of the front line," reports the *Oberkommando der Wehrmacht,* the army's high command.

Rommel's *Afrika Korps,* which had been advancing toward Cairo, is repelled and destroyed. Death announcements take up more and more space in the newspapers: "My son (father, husband) has given his life for the *Führer* and *Vaterland.*" My own father is wounded near Stalingrad.

The Allied air forces pound Germany, first by night, but soon by day also. Stuttgart, where we live, has become a major target. Our cellar, although newly fitted with steel doors and strong upright beams to strengthen the ceiling, can no longer withstand the exploding bombs. The people dig *Stollen,* tunnels, into the hills that surround the beautiful city. In our *Stollen,* a five-minute walk from our house, close to a thousand people find protection. Almost every night, sometimes two or three times, we must leave our beds and crawl like moles into the cold, damp, underground shelter. On a rare night when the sirens do not jolt us from sleep, my two-year-old cousin, Lore, who lives upstairs, wakes up and pleads with her mother: "*Stollen gehen!* Go to the tunnel! *Komm Stollen gehen!*"

Tante Mina, as well as Rosa and Frieda and their husbands, have all become homeless but are alive. My Carle grandparents' house is also destroyed, but they, too, have survived. Our house, damaged but still standing, is surrounded by many ruins. Eventually, half of Stuttgart will have been reduced to rubble. An American Flying Fortress, smoke streaming from its engines, streaks across the sky above our house before exploding a few miles away.

My school building hasn't been hit yet (that will come later); schooling is fragmentary at best. But I still like to draw and paint. Caught up in the spirit of the times, I draw tanks and fighter planes with exotic armament. And I still look forward to an occasional art class with *Herr* Krauss, my art teacher.

One day, *Herr* Krauss invites me to his house. On the appointed day, I get on my bicycle and pedal to his place on the outskirts of town. He tells me that he likes the freedom and sketchy quality of my work. The trouble is that according to state regulations, he is supposed to teach us naturalism and realism, and to discourage such

Stuttgart destroyed

My art teacher Herr Fridolin Krauss

tendencies as my loose handling of my drawings. He goes to a hiding place and from it pulls out a neatly wrapped box. My art teacher unwraps this box and opens it to show me the reproductions of works of "forbidden art" done by so-called "degenerate artists"—Picasso, Klee, Matisse, Braque, Kandinsky, and examples of German Expressionism. These are names I have never heard, pictures I did not know existed. Their strange beauty almost blinds me. "Don't tell anyone what you have seen today," warns *Herr* Krauss. "Just remember their free and loose style."

Many schools in heavily bombed areas have already been evacuated, and in 1943 the word is passed around that our school, too, will be evacuated soon. The children will be sent to safer areas. One day, on short notice, all the pupils and teachers are put on a train. An anti-aircraft cannon is mounted on the last car in place of a caboose. Most trains, passenger and freight, civilian and military, now have four-barreled antiaircraft guns that swivel in all directions.

We arrive at an undamaged railroad station—*Schwenningen,* declares a sign. It is a small town at the edge of the Black Forest in the southwest corner of Germany. A welcoming committee, local children with small hand-pulled wagons, hand out slips of paper with names penciled on them. My piece of paper has *Gutekunst* written on it. Appropriately, the name means "good art"! One of the local boys throws my suitcase onto his wagon, then, he pulling and I pushing, we move away from the station through the streets of a lovely small town without ruins, rubble, or boarded-up windows. The air smells sweet; I almost miss the smell of burnt wood doused by water that now characterizes Stuttgart.

I am taken to the home of the family to whom I have been assigned. *Herr* Gutekunst, a portly man with short white hair, is stern but fair-minded. *Frau* Gutekunst has kind and expressive eyes. I respond to her warmth like a dried-up sponge dipped into a pail of water. Never before have I known a woman with such an inner glow; I begin to trust and love her, step-by-step. They have two daughters. Annemarie is my age, and Ruth is a few years younger. Hans, their son, is away at the front. The authorities have decreed that his room shall be mine for the duration of the war.

They live in a comfortable house with elegant furniture and fine rugs. Next to their modern kitchen is the *Bauernstube,* a room furnished with a rustic corner bench and a heavy wooden table that must have come from an ancient farmhouse. An antique painted cupboard stands in the corner. On the wall hang a cuckoo clock, a pipe collection, engraved pewter plates, and the stuffed head of a stag with antlers.

With Mathilde, my first girlfriend

This is to be my new home. I am not treated like an intruder but like a newfound brother and son. Only Hans, when he comes home on one of his occasional furloughs, eyes me with suspicion.

School here, too, is very confusing. We share the classrooms in shifts with the local students and with a second group of evacuees from another city. During the winter the school is closed altogether due to the lack of heating fuel. We are expected to do our schoolwork at home. Spot checks by our teachers are threatened. But our teachers, tired and beyond retirement age, are easily outfoxed. My already shaky education is taking another nosedive.

Boys sixteen years old are already in uniform, serving as *Flakhelfer*, auxiliary antiaircraft crews, and those seventeen and older are at the Russian front or some far-flung outpost of German expansion. This situation leaves fourteen-and fifteen-year-old boys—I was now fifteen—to be the "men" of the town.

At a local concert, unable to view the musicians, I lean slightly to my right. A young woman next to me, whose view is also obstructed, leans slightly to her left. A strand of her hair brushes gently against my cheek, and a hint of her warmth radiates toward me. After the concert, we walk through the darkened streets until we reach her house, where we shake hands. She is eighteen years old, has large brown eyes and dark hair, which sharply contrast with her white skin. We meet again and again. We walk through the fields, along the river, and under trees until the sun sets. New, undefined feelings take hold of me, slowly and irresistibly.

"Do you like me?" she asks me one day. I nod.

"Close your eyes," she tells me. Her lips press against mine. When we meet again, I ask her if she likes me. And I kiss her back.

"Do you love me?" she asks this time. I nod.

"Close your eyes and part your lips—just a little."

When we were evacuated, it was to save the future generation. But the times are changing, the tide of battle has turned against Germany. Desperation has set in. We children are again put on a train. This train, which has been raked with bullets from low-flying Allied fighter planes, resembles a sieve. Seats and window-panes are nonexistent. We travel by night because it is no longer possible to travel by day. The Allied forces have absolute supremacy in the air; they shoot at anything, anytime. After repeated switchings of route, stopping by day to hide in abandoned buildings, we are deposited at the Siegfried Line, alongside the Rhine River. In the distance we hear artillery fire. Russian and Italian prisoners of war, Polish "slave workers," and old German men dig trenches, side by side. We join them in this work. But everything seems disorganized. No one is in charge of us boys. When the others are fed, we discover that no rations have been allotted for us. We are hungry, some of us are ill with diarrhea or other ailments. Finally, several of the prisoners of war share their meager rations with us.

As I clean out my mess kit in the Rhine after our meal, spurts of water erupt in front of me as if from an underwater fountain. I am puzzled. Sound travels very slowly: a machine gun-firing Mustang swoops past and pulls back up into the sky. Three men near me collapse in their blood and die. I develop sores on one of my legs and spend a few days in a makeshift hospital before I receive orders to return to Stuttgart.

I won't remember much of how I manage to get home. But I recall more Mustang attacks as I follow twisted railroad tracks, walk around bomb craters, pick up a ride on an open truck. Finally, I arrive in Stuttgart.

Hitler is still threatening to annihilate the Bolsheviks and the Capitalists with his "secret weapon." The Allied forces and the Russians have crossed into Germany.

Before long, a Nazi in an official brown shirt knocks at our door. My mother responds and stands in the doorway listening to him.

"Your son will report for duty tomorrow morning at the plaza in front of the railroad station."

"*Jawohl,* very well," replies my mother.

"He will be issued a *Panzerfaust,* a bazooka, to defend the *Vaterland.*"

"*Jawohl.*"

"He will bring with him an extra set of under-wear and a blanket."

"*Jawohl.*"

But the next morning, my mother refuses to let me go. My dreams of becoming a war hero are crushed. Boys fourteen and fifteen years old who do report for duty the next day retreat with the army toward Bavaria. When they are finally confronted by American soldiers in Sherman tanks, they panic and run. Nazi storm troopers hang several of these young "deserters" as a warning to others.

During the night a few artillery shells hit our fire station, then everything is unusually quiet. In the morning we see white bed sheets hanging from windows. French colonial soldiers are marching through the streets! One of them relieves me of my watch and my shoes. The war is over. Germany capitulates. It is springtime, 1945. My father is missing in action.

1945–1946. Still there has been no word from my father. A network of rumors has spread across the land. Someone has told somebody that my father is somewhere in Russia, and somehow this message is relayed to us. Almost a year later, we receive a postcard containing twenty-five words—the limit permitted—from a POW camp deep inside Russia. My father is alive!

Professor Ernst Schneidler

For some months following the end of the war, our school remained closed. The girls' wing had sustained a direct bomb hit and was a heap of steel girders and broken stone.

I found a job as a file clerk with the Denazification Department of the United States Military Government. From this job I derived two overdue benefits. One, I learned to speak English again, and, two, I was permitted to eat in the United States officers' dining room. To be able to eat with the officers was akin to having arrived in paradise. Quickly my thin features began to round out. During these meals, I surreptitiously stuffed peanut butter sandwiches, lumps of butter, cubes of sugar, leftover bits of steak, and desserts into my pockets. I also emptied the ashtrays of cigarette butts, as the tobacco gained from the butts had become the currency of the local black market where scarce foodstuff was sold. My family—remember, four floors of them—awaited my return each evening with anxious eyes.

But after a few short months of this, school reopened and I had to leave my Garden of Eden. Now I disliked school more than ever. I found it hard to follow instructions; math and Latin were torture; I couldn't distinguish between chemistry, biology, and physics. Everything was slightly blurred. Partly as escape, I visited the library across from the school for the first time. The library, too, had broken walls, waterstained ceilings, and boarded-up windows. But there, a kind librarian, with an old coat over her thin shoulders, introduced me to Franz Kafka, Thomas Mann, and André Gide, all forbidden authors just a short time earlier. I am not sure that I understood the deeper meanings of all

their writings, but, with the librarian gently urging me on, I absorbed the heartbeat of every page.

Art classes still held the greatest interest for me. I asked *Herr* Krauss to tell me which professions in the art field were open to me. He recommended that I study commercial art in the graphic arts department of the *Akademie der bildenden Künste* in Stuttgart under the guidance of Professor Ernst Schneidler, who offered classes in book and advertising design, poster art, illustration, calligraphy, typography, photography, and other related courses.

My Oelschläger grandfather, who owned a small tool and die factory, had taken it upon himself during my father's absence to guide me toward a respectable future. Sitting in my room "doing pictures" was clearly not a part of his plans for me.

"Why not become an engineer?" he offered. "Then one day you can inherit the factory."

"No."

oppose my choice. And I knew that my father would have approved wholeheartedly.

"Then at least think about becoming a dentist," he persisted. "Imagine, people will then call you *'Herr Doktor.'*"

"No."

Fortunately, my mother, remembering and honoring the words of my early teacher, did not

The *Akademie* had been closed for about two years because of the war and the destruction that the building itself had suffered. Only a few rooms here and there had been poorly repaired. Now a stream of former soldiers, and men and women who had been unable to study heretofore, as well as members of the newer generation, like myself, were eager to be admitted. About three hundred people applied to the graphic arts department alone, of which one hundred or so were given a test, and around fifty of those finally accepted. Each student who had been accepted was also required to work several hundred hours under the guidance of a professional construction crew in restoring the structure to a halfway tolerable condition.

Professor Schneidler looked at my work and accepted me without the test that the others had to take. I was sixteen years old, two years below the minimum age. I was so impressed with myself that I took on the mannerisms and behavior that I imagined artists possessed: I wore a wild scarf around my neck and perched a rakish beret on top of my unruly hair. I affected certain nervous movements—sometimes, as I was walking down the street, I would suddenly

A sketch for an Edgar Allan Poe story

stop, stretch out my arms, and with my two hands frame a scene like a famous film director.

One day Professor Schneidler asked me to come to his office. "*Herr* Carle," he said with his crisp Prussian officer's voice (he had served in World War I), "you are the least talented student that I have taught in forty years of teaching!"

I was stunned.

"You are expelled," he added.

The next morning I knocked meekly at his door, hoping against hope that somehow I would be able to turn this matter around.

"Come in."

Cautiously, I stuck my head through the doorway.

"You can stay," he told me, politely gesturing to me to sit down. "For the next three semesters you will be not an artist, but an apprentice in the typesetting department."

Schneidler was a most remarkable teacher. His students, past and present, respected him deeply and called him simply *Meister*. A true master, he discovered each individual's talent and cultivated it. He channeled my vanity, which ultimately would have been destructive, into a constructive energy. The discipline of setting type by hand and the inherent rules and limita-tions of typography have shaped my approach to my work ever since. I was later readmitted to regular art and design classes. My four years at the *Akademie* were inspiring and exhilarating. Ten stifling years at the grammar and high

Collage poster design

29

schools were behind me at last, to be recalled only in my nightmares.

In the last year of my studies I was commissioned to design posters for *Amerika Haus*, the United States Information Center. Mr. Lovegrove, the United States cultural attaché, allowed me total freedom in my designs, and I completed a series of posters of which I am still proud.

Schneidler's students were sought after and were often hired by advertising agencies, publishers, and graphics studios even before they had graduated. In this way, without having to search for a job, I became the art director of the promotion department for a fashion magazine. In 1952, after two years of experience as a graphic designer and poster artist in Germany, I felt ready to return to the United States. I was not yet twenty-three years old, but I had a nice portfolio and forty dollars in my pocket.

While I was still studying, my father had returned from the prisoner-of-war camp in Russia in late 1947. He arrived in rags, weighing a mere eighty pounds, and shaking with malaria. He was a broken man, both physically and emotionally, who would never really recover or "belong" to our family again. My mother and I had managed without him for eight long years. He and I could not reestablish our once close and warm relationship. I had grown up and was stepping out into the world, a new world, while he barely held on to life.

When I last saw him, during a visit to Germany years later, in 1959, he was on his way to the hospital, where he would die. We stood together at the railroad station, not knowing what to say to each other. In my mind I recalled the happiness he had offered me in my early childhood, when he passed on to me his dreams, which he had not been able to fulfill for himself.

My first commercial assignment—a poster for the U.S. Information Center, linocut, 1950

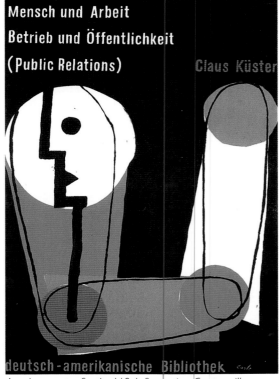

Another poster for the U.S. Information Center, silk screen

I landed in New York on a beautiful day in May of 1952. The sky was a bright blue, without a cloud in sight, and I felt that I had come home. I stayed briefly with an uncle, my father's younger brother, and his family in the Bronx; then I was offered the chance to "apartment-sit" in a building near Broadway and 57th Street. Now I had to look for a job.

Someone suggested that I should go to see the Annual New York Art Directors' Show. There my eyes fell on some exciting designs for *Fortune* magazine. "Leo Lionni, Art Director," it said on a small sticker next to the design. I went immediately to a phone booth, looked up the number for the magazine, "JU 6-1212," I still remember, and called Mr. Lionni. I explained to him that I had seen his work and that I liked it and that perhaps he'd like my work, too, and that I had just come from Germany.

"Come tomorrow morning at eleven," a deep, sonorous voice told me.

Next day, a swift and silent elevator took me to one of the top floors of Rockefeller Center. A receptionist escorted me to a spacious, modern office overlooking the city. Leo Lionni, a tall, handsome, well-dressed man with horn-rimmed glasses and an encouraging smile, shook my hand. He seemed to like my work and offered me a job. Not with *Fortune* magazine, but to assist him with his freelance work, which he did from a small studio around the corner near Saks Fifth Avenue.

"What salary would you like to have?"

My father's forty dollars came to mind. "Forty dollars a week."

"No, no. I'd pay you at least a hundred dollars."

One more poster for the U.S. Information Center, silk screen

As an art student

"No, no. You can't do that."

"Oh, yes, I can," he said, looking at his wrist-watch. It was twelve o'clock, and he invited me, together with his assistant, Walter Allner, for lunch. We went to an elegant Italian restaurant, where we were greeted like old friends. The waiters fussed over Mr. Lionni and his guests. The meal was delicious. And Mr. Lionni left a generous tip as we left—it would have made a great dent in my own pocketbook, I thought.

When we returned to his office, Leo Lionni told me that since the job he had offered to me would mean that I'd be the only person in that studio, he thought I might feel lonely.

"You should be out with people, making friends, learning the language." He reached for his telephone and had a brief conversation. "I have made an appointment for you. Here," he said, and gave me a note. "George Krikorian, Art Director, Promotion Department, *The New York Times*," he had written. There was an address and a telephone number. "This would be a good job for you," said Lionni, "but if it doesn't work out, my offer is still good."

I left my portfolio at Mr. Krikorian's office. Later in the day he called and asked me to come in for an interview. Before I went to see him, I excitedly called Lionni about the pending meeting.

"Before you go," he said, "come and see me."

Again I took the wonderful elevator to Leo Lionni's office.

"If Krikorian wants to hire you, and if you're asked how much you'd like to earn, you tell him one hundred dollars per week."

"Oh, I can't do that."

"If you don't, I'll never speak to you again!"

Mr. Krikorian seemed interested in hiring me. "How much would you like to earn?" he inquired.

I swallowed, then whispered, "One hundred dollars a week."

"Would you start for eighty-five?"

"Yes, yes!" I shouted.

Just two weeks before, I had arrived in New York. Now I had a fine job; I liked my work, my colleagues, and *The New York Times* cafeteria.

Five months later, Uncle Sam sent me his greetings, inviting me to participate in sixteen exciting weeks of basic training at Fort Dix, New Jersey. And so began my soldier's career.

A whistle blew, and all the new recruits in their stiff and ill-fitting uniforms rushed from the barracks and stood in formation: "Het, hut!" ordered Sergeant Schmidt. I had not understood that "Het, hut!" means "Attention!" and continued to stand, hands in my pocket, looking around, while all the others had come to attention.

"You!"

"Yes."

"Yes, Sergeant," said Sergeant Schmidt correcting me.

"Yes, Sergeant."

"Give me twenty."

"Twenty what?"

"I'll show you," said Sergeant Schmidt, demonstrating the art of the push-up.

Doing push-ups looks deceptively easy to those who have never done any.

I soon learned to obey Sergeant Schmidt, who one day, upon discovering that I had been brought up in Germany, barked at me, "I always thought that the Germans were good soldiers. What kind of a German are you, anyway?" and with that, he proceeded to tear my bunk bed apart.

I also learned to obey the large sign above the dining hall—Take All You Want, Eat All You Take—and gained many pounds despite rigorous marches at all times during the day and night, push-ups, kitchen duty, guard duty, climbing ropes, crawling on my hands and knees across the parade grounds, and more push-ups. I met young Americans from all walks of life and enjoyed and appreciated their friendship. My English improved so much that, while on a weekend pass visiting friends in New York, I amazed them by the number of swearwords I had added to my vocabulary.

Toward the end of basic training we were asked who of us had a knowledge of a foreign language.

In the U.S. Army, 1952

I raised my hand. The German test had been geared for Americans, so naturally I passed the test with flying colors. Within a short time I found myself with many other new soldiers on a tiny troop transport, battling the waves of the North Atlantic. I was on my way back to Germany! I reported for duty with the Second Armored Division, named "Hell on Wheels."

"Can you drive a truck?" asked the company commander.

"No, sir."

"What do you know about artillery?"

"Nothing, sir." I had been trained in the infantry.

"You will be the mail clerk."

"Yes, sir."

Cirsten and Rolf, grown up

Later, I was assigned to special services of the Seventh United States Army in Stuttgart. An understanding captain accepted my proposal that I should not need a bunk in the barracks. At five each afternoon I put on my civilian suit and took the trolley car to my old house and slept in my old bed. My mother served me breakfast before I rushed back to the U.S. Army.

On leave on a weekend pass in Wiesbaden, I ran into a former colleague from my days with the German fashion magazine. My colleague had her younger sister, Dorothea Wohlenberg, with her. A year later, in 1954, Dorothea, nineteen years old, and I, twenty-five, were married, just shortly before my discharge. A month later my young bride followed me to New York, where I had resumed my old job with *The New York Times*. Two years later I became an art director for an advertising agency that specialized in pharmaceutical advertising.

First Dorothea and I lived in Queens in a large apartment building. Cirsten, our first child, was about two years old when we moved to a house in Irvington-on-Hudson. There our son, Rolf, was born. When Cirsten and Rolf were six and four years old, Dorothea and I separated and were eventually divorced. This simple sentence cannot begin to convey my pain and anguish at this breakup.

For the next ten years I remained a bachelor. On weekends and vacations my children visited me in my studio apartment—a fourth-floor walk-up in a charming old brownstone on 12th Street in Greenwich Village. Before going to bed my children delighted in running back and forth the length of my apartment, about forty feet.

Invariably Mrs. Simpson from downstairs called up to complain about the noise. I tried to explain to her that I was a weekend father. I pleaded with her for some understanding, since this happened only once a week for a few minutes. But the following weekend, Mrs. Simpson called again.

"Isn't there anything you can do to make your children be quiet, Mr. Carle?"

"Yes, Mrs. Simpson," I said reasonably. "I shall line them up and shoot them."

After that Mrs. Simpson became our best friend. She brought gifts for my children, asked if she could baby-sit, and, best of all, encouraged them to run back and forth the length of my apartment to their hearts' content.

At about the same time as the separation between Dorothea and me took place, I had quit my job with the advertising agency in order to freelance as a graphic designer and illustrator in the field of advertising. I had come to the conclusion that I didn't want to sit in meetings, write memos, entertain clients, and catch commuter trains. I simply wanted to create pictures .

One day, a fateful day for me, a publisher of so-called educational materials for preschool and primary-grade children asked me to illustrate one of their projects. But the project was poorly conceived and uninspiring. It reminded me of the German schoolroom of my childhood, with the small windows and hard pencils. "The project was scientifically designed by educational experts," I was told. Still, I knew that it wouldn't work, that children would be bored by it just as the child in me was.

But shortly afterward, Dr. Bill Martin Jr, writer, editor, and educator, asked me to illustrate his manuscript *Brown Bear, Brown Bear, What Do You See?* What an inspiring approach! Now the large sheets of paper, the colorful paints and fat brushes of my earlier American school came to my mind. I was set on fire! It was possible, after all, to do something special, something that would show a child the joy to be found in books.

With Bill Martin Jr on the occasion of the 25th anniversary of Brown Bear, Brown Bear, What Do You See?

After seeing this illustration for an advertisement, Bill Martin Jr asked me to illustrate his story

Sometime later, a publisher asked me to illustrate a historical cookbook. I chose to do it in linoleum cuts. I delivered the illustrations to Ann Beneduce, the editor, and she and I began to talk about books in general and about picture books in particular. I told her about some of my rough ideas, which by now were filling up a small cardboard box. I also confessed to Ann that at the age of six I had stopped paying attention to grammar, spelling, and punctuation. "I am not interested in grammar, spelling, and punctuation," said Ann. "I am interested in ideas."

However, to be on the safe side, I submitted a wordless book—*1, 2, 3 to the Zoo*. And soon, to my surprise, I found a contract for that book in my mailbox. Encouraged, I next submitted a story about a bookworm, whom I had changed into a green worm, who had eaten holes through apples, pears, and chocolate cake.

"I'm not so sure about a green worm," said

My sister Christa, who is 21 years younger than I, 1959:
The Very Hungry Caterpillar *is dedicated to her*

Ann. We then discussed other animals and insects, that might be more appealing and more appropriate.

"How about a caterpillar?" remarked Ann after a while.

"Butterfly!" I exclaimed without a moment's hesitation.

And so *The Very Hungry Caterpillar* was launched. Almost without planning it, I had become an author and illustrator of books for young children. From then on I began to devote all my time to picture books.

A special relationship between author and editor is crucial to the success of a book. Ann's and my "caterpillar and butterfly" exchange has become symbolic of a working relationship that operates on the same wavelength and is marked by deep mutual respect and affection. Neither of us has ever imposed his or her will upon the other. An organic and easy flow of ideas, just plain talking and a lot of listening to each other, has given birth to many books since we first met. In that way some ideas have also faded away—quietly and peacefully, without a rejection slip.

I didn't realize it clearly then, but my life was beginning to move onto its true course. The long, dark time of growing up in wartime Germany, the cruelly enforced discipline of my school years there, the dutifully performed work at my jobs in advertising—all these were finally losing their rigid grip on me. The child inside me—who had been so suddenly and sharply uprooted and repressed—was beginning to come joyfully back to life.

With my wife, Barbara

I remembered those who had helped me along the way, even in those nightmare days in Hitler's Germany: the art teacher who had risked his life to show me forbidden art; the librarian who revealed to me that books contained not just work and words, but wisdom and joy; my foster mother, *Frau* Gutekunst, who opened her generous heart to me; the prisoner of war who shared his food with me, showing me that no human being is an enemy; my father, who taught me to love the world of nature; my own children, who helped revive in me my own early childhood happiness; Professor Schneidler, who taught me the discipline that beauty requires of its creators; Leo Lionni, Bill Martin Jr, and especially Ann Beneduce, who showed me that I could make a living as an artist. These and others had led me to the turning point at which I found myself.

From then on, I began to neglect my other work. From then on, I began to work on books for children and for the child in me. From then on, I began to work on books that were to fulfill my own needs—needs that had gone unfulfilled for so long.

My early background as a graphic designer and my later interest in picture books now fell into place. The graphic designer wanted to push paper and print to their limits for the sake of creativity, interest, and intrigue. The storyteller wanted to create a touchable book that was also a readable toy, to make that very first day in school just a little bit easier.

After my divorce, I was sure that I would not marry again. But one day, I invited Barbara Morrison, a friend I had not seen for two years,

for dinner. When she arrived, she presented me with one single-stemmed anthurium, wrapped loosely in a white, translucent paper. A year and a half later, in 1973, we happily exchanged marriage vows.

Barbara's work and mine have much in common. I feel that we all have our handicaps, some small, some large; and through my books I attempt to address these needs. Barbara, as an educator, worked directly with children who had special needs, and with their parents.

In 1974, we moved from New York City to a new house on fifty beautiful acres in the Berkshire mountains, in the northwest corner of Massachusetts, overlooking a meadow, trees, and distant hills. Recently, after having lost some of our initial enthusiasm for our isolated life on a windswept hill in the winter, we purchased an older house in nearby Northampton, to spend the winter near shops, friends, movie houses, a library, a Chinese restaurant, and the post office—all within walking distance.

Hawley, Massachusetts house in the summertime

Northampton house in the wintertime

Central to my work is this: I am fascinated by the period in a child's life when he or she, for the first time, leaves home to go to school. What a gulf a child must cross then: from home and security, a world of play and the senses, to a world of reason and abstraction, order and discipline. I should like my books to bridge that great divide. Some of my books have holes, cutouts, flaps to lift, or a raised, touchable surface. They are half toy (home) and half book (school). A book that can be touched and felt, a toy that can be read. And, indeed, don't we speak of grasping an idea, or of being in touch with our feelings!

I attempt to have many levels in my books: funny animals, exciting colors, a story, humor, entertainment, mystery, emotional content—and learning. Depending on the child's interest, ability, or curiosity, he or she can select the level where he or she feels comfortable. Some of these levels can and should be demanding and challenging. We just as often fail to address the "gifted" child as we neglect the "slow" child.

In *The Grouchy Ladybug,* for instance, in addition to the obvious, basic story of how the quarreling bugs make peace, there is a harder, more subtle lesson about how the rising and the setting of the sun are correlated to time. I can well imagine a child, perhaps one in a thousand, who will be intrigued enough to ask why the sun and time do relate to each other in this way. I can also imagine a sensitive adult, perhaps also one in a thousand, who will initiate a conversation with that child about our earth in the great design of the universe. There are many kinds of young readers; each one is an individual and finds something different, something special, in a book.

In the task which I have set out to do, I sometimes feel exhilarated, at other times frustrated. Sometimes I feel that I am a great success, at other times that I am the worst of failures. But this simply means that one is living and growing within one's wide range of emotions.

Most picture books have thirty-two pages, and I take great care within this space as to how I place the pictures, how I develop and pace the ideas and images, and how the story should end. A book needs to be composed like a symphony, a duet, or a quiet piece of chamber music. A style and flow must be established. But most of all, one should have an open mind and listen to one's intuition: the unexplainable, the coincidental, even the quirky. Look at the crack in the ceiling and see it take on a shape and a voice.

My work has brought me in touch with children in many countries. I have spoken and read to, drawn for, and entertained children across the United States, and also in England, Scotland, Holland, Germany, Finland, Italy, Mexico, Japan, and once in a bookstore in Paris. And I am grateful that so many children in so many countries have embraced my books, that they write me their funny, sad, touching, and sometimes routine letters. I think that the following note, scribbled in tiny letters, which were squeezed into the upper corner of the page, makes a fitting ending to my story.

Dear Eric,
You draw good. I like your pictures.
Our teacher made us read all your books.
Will you ever retire?
Love, Jennifer

Ann Beneduce
IT TAKES THE PRACTICED HAND

Today, Eric Carle is known around the world for his beautiful and highly original picture books for children. But this was not always so. I well remember my first introduction to his work. On the front of the brochure I was examining, "think big," whispered a blue whale, whose huge form swept in streamlined curves across a double spread. Revealed by a turn of the page, "THINK SMALL," shouted a tiny red ladybug. I was excited to see how perfectly the design, the bright colors, and the directness of the art expressed the succinct message. It was a promotion piece from a newcomer in the children's book field, a talented young artist named Eric Carle. My art director, Jack Jaget, thought we should give him an assignment. I heartily agreed, and we commissioned him to illustrate an unusual cookbook[1] we were publishing. When he brought in his finished art, eighty-five stunning linocuts, I was so impressed that I urged him to let me see more of his work.

Ms. Ann Beneduce was the first editor to publish books with Eric's story and illustrations. Ann has become a longtime friend who worked with Eric on over twenty books.

The next week, he brought in his portfolio and, over lunch, we talked with growing excitement about his ideas. His blue-gray eyes sparkled, and an unruly lock of light brown hair kept springing up as he gestured animatedly. A slight trace of a German accent reminded me that, although born in the United States, he had lived for many years in Germany, where he had received most of his education as well as his art training. Now a successful art director for a large New York advertising agency, he had recently also illustrated several books for children, books written by various authors. Although none of these projects had seemed to him entirely fulfilling, a seed had been planted—a tiny seed that was to grow and become an enormous and beautiful flower. He had particularly enjoyed illustrating *Brown Bear, Brown Bear, What Do You See?* by Bill Martin Jr. The rhythmic text with its warm, appealing message struck a responsive chord in him. Now he wanted to do some books that would be totally his own creations, both as to story and to illustrations. It was as if a door in his psyche had suddenly opened and through it Eric Carle had begun to reach back into his inner self, traveling back in time through his life, past his adult career, his marriage and family, his art training, his schooling, back at last to his own childhood experiences and emotions. He was eager to share these newly rediscovered feelings and ideas with children.

His enthusiasm was contagious. He had already filled a large cardboard box with sketches and ideas for picture books. "Send me some," I urged him—and before long there appeared on my desk the first draft of what would become Eric Carle's first original picture book, *1, 2,3 to the Zoo*. It was clear to me at once that an enormously talented artist had burst upon the children's book scene. The artwork was brilliant, executed in a collage of painted, multicolored tissues, cut and layered to achieve rich colors and subtle textures. The eye-catching jacket design, with the title printed across the open jaws of a lion, reflected Carle's early career as a poster artist. Indeed, his unique ability to distill the essence of his message was evident on every bravura double-spread. The pictures were so eloquent that there was no need for any text at all—the numerals for counting the animals as they rode to the zoo, plus the small diagrams showing the accumulation of creatures on the train, were enough to convey the learning information, while the wordless storyline was easily followed in striking double spread illustrations, ending in a gatefold page that opened out dramatically to show the festive final scene (with the ever-present little mouse scurrying into the zoo along with the other animals!).

The next book that Eric Carle created was *The Very Hungry Caterpillar*, the book that made him famous and is still his most beloved work. In this book, many of the things that we now think of as characteristic of his work appeared: his "warm grasp of the subject matter,"[2] presenting an abstract or general idea through a particular story and an individual character; his deep empathy with nature (i.e. animals, plants, and insects) as well as his interest in natural

Linocut from Red Flannel Hash and Shoo-fly Pie

processes and events; his eagerness to share with children the joy of learning; his innovative approach to bookmaking, using die-cut holes and different-sized pages to make his points clearer and more dramatic; and, of course, his dazzling art techniques and effects.

The artwork in *The Very Hungry Caterpillar* is much richer than that in his previous books. Thus, in the opening spread, showing the egg on a leaf by the light of the moon, he has used almost the entire page, "bleeding" (that is, without margins) on three sides, in a poetic, painterly, and quasi-realistic scene. The next spread, by contrast, is strongly stylized, with the tiny caterpillar and the enormous, smiling sun appearing like images from the ritual art of some primitive culture. On the next spread, yet more surprises appear: the cutoff pages with die-cut holes invite small fingers to poke through and follow the path of the hungry caterpillar as he eats his way through fruits

and sweets and other delicacies. Readers can also learn the days of the week in sequence and trace the life cycle of the butterfly, a radiant creature that emerges triumphantly on the last spread. Nothing is accidental—every word and every picture is carefully chosen or planned—yet so accomplished is the artist's technique that it has all the exhilaration of something completely spontaneous. The endpapers, with white dots scattered seemingly at random on multicolored patches, are wonderful examples of modern abstract art; yet they really represent the holes eaten by the caterpillar. On the title page, the dots appear again, but now in color and lined up in a strongly controlled design.

Naturally, all of this did not emerge full-blown from the head of its creator. The simplicity and naturalness of Eric Carle's finished work makes it appear to have been created without effort. But this is not the case. Nearly all of his books require months or even years of thought, of

1 2 3

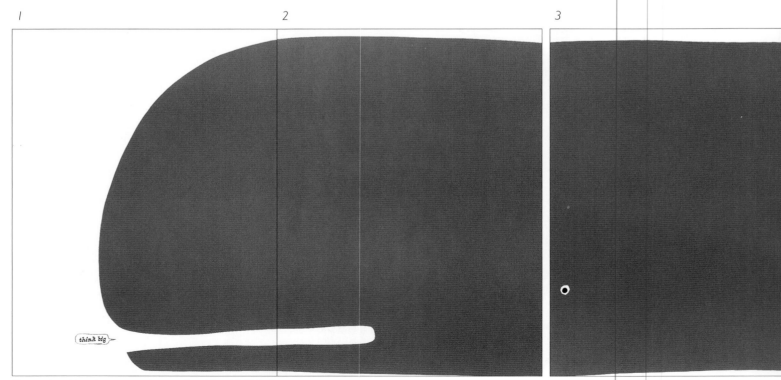

Promotional brochure: actual page size 10 x 13 ½ inches

trial and error, of research and experiment. Beginning with the early books and continuing throughout many years that followed, a wonderfully fruitful relationship developed between artist and editor, as well as a warm and enduring friendship. A free and open exchange of ideas flowed between us, allowing me to share to a rare degree in the artist's creative process. My participation was, of course, vicarious—the creativity was always his. But my experience as an editor and publisher, my sense of the needs of both the marketplace and (more importantly to both of us) of the young children for whom the books were intended made my input valuable to him. My role was a catalytic or enabling one. As his editor, I had first to understand and appreciate what it was that he wished to express, and then to ensure that this was expressed in the best possible way. Then, too, I had to produce the books, nearly every one of which offered some new and formidable challenge to the manufacturers.

The Very Hungry Caterpillar was a product of this kind of cooperation between artist and editor and offers a good example of our working process. When Eric Carle first brought this story in, it was actually called *A Week with Willi Worm* and it was about a little green worm that ate its way through books and other indigestible fare. The wonderful endpapers were there, and the die-cut pages, and it was obvious that it contained the germ of a brilliant book. But something more was needed. As we talked, the ideas began to grow. "I'm not so sure about a green worm as a central character," I said. "How about, say, a caterpillar?" "A butterfly!" exclaimed Eric, picking up on the idea and carrying it to its perfect conclusion. Before long, he had worked out all the details of the story and jubilantly delivered the final art and the intricate dummy for the book. It was clearly a masterpiece, but to my dismay, I could not find a printer or a binder in the United States at that time who could produce it! By good luck, I was

4 5 6

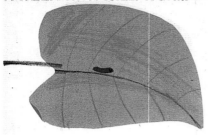

A WEEK WITH WILLI WORM A COUNTIN BOOK BY ERIC CARLE

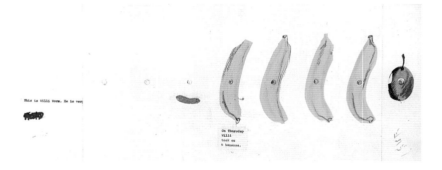

This is Willi Worm. He is very hungry. He hasn't eaten through anything for a long time.

This is Willi Worm. He is very

On Thursday
Willi
took on
4 bananas,

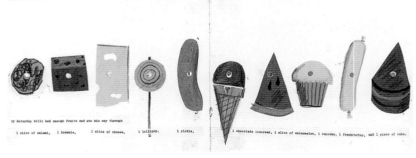

On Saturday Willi had enough fruits and ate his way through

1 slice of salami,   1 brownie,   1 slice of cheese,   1 lollipop,   1 pickle,   1 chocolate icecream, 1 slice of watermelon, 1 cupcake, 1 frankfurter, and 1 piece of cake.

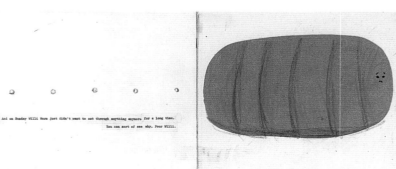

And on Sunday Willi Worm just didn't want to eat through anything anymore for a long time.

You can sort of see why. Poor Willi.

A Week with Willi Worm, *the precursor to* The Very Hungry Caterpillar

invited to visit Japan for a few weeks in the summer of 1968. It was intended as a holiday, but I couldn't resist taking Eric's project along with me and showing it to some of the Japanese publishers. One of these, Hiroshi Imamura, the president of the distinguished firm of Kaisei-Sha Publishing, fell in love with the book, too, and offered to find a way to produce it for me. And so it was that, with his help, *The Very Hungry Caterpillar* finally appeared in 1969, first in the United States and soon thereafter in England and in Japan, to universal acclaim.

The enormous popularity of this book with young readers and their parents is gratifying but almost puzzling to its creator, who professes to be fonder of some of his later books than of this one. But *The Very Hungry Caterpillar* has eaten its way into the hearts of small readers in a score of countries all around the world and has been translated into as many languages. It is certainly one of the best-known and most widely loved of all contemporary children's stories.

Since that book appeared, Eric Carle has continued to create beautiful and highly original picture books for children. Many employ devices such as cutout shapes;[3] split pages;[4] movable parts;[5] leporello or accordion folding;[6] gatefolds or other complex folds;[7] odd-sized pages;[8] raised, tactile images;[9] and even strings for moving animal characters or other things through the die-cut pages of a book.[10] But these devices are always germane to the message or story of the book. They are never extraneous gadgetry. His artwork, though he usually continues to use his painted and layered cutouts and collages, has grown in subtlety and expressiveness. Some-times the collages are accented with crayon or,

With Ann Beneduce in her office

more frequently now, with acrylic. In fact, in some of his books, such as *Animals Animals* and *A House for Hermit Crab*, the endpapers are done entirely in acrylic in a strikingly free, modern, and very painterly style. Comparing his recent works with his earlier books, one can see a vast difference, a deepening and enrichment in his handling of textures and images; yet each one is unmistakably Eric Carle's.

The simplicity of his style is deceptive. It takes the practiced hand to make the simple gesture. In addition to its technical brilliance, Eric Carle's work derives its power from the artist's depth of involvement with his subject matter. This involvement is both emotional and intellectual. Like the colored tissues he uses in his collages, ideas and emotions are layered in his memory, forming rich textures. These are the materials with which he works, shaping them carefully to his own point of view. Ideas and visual images become stories and illustrations, expressed in clear, simple words and boldly designed forms, taking their places in compositions that seem simultaneously controlled and free, perfectly in balance and inevitably right.

One of the things that first attracted me to Eric Carle's work was not only the beauty but also the expressiveness of his graphic style. He can compress a very complex idea into a simple, direct image. Even a very small child can grasp his meaning instantly. This leads to the other characteristic that makes his work so powerful —his respect for the child who will read the book and look at the pictures in it. He remembers vividly his own childhood experiences of the joy of learning and creativity. He believes that young children really want to explore their

world and that they enjoy making learning discoveries on their own. His books, therefore, while aesthetically pleasing and entertaining, always also offer the child the opportunity to learn something of real interest and value. This unique combintion of beautiful form and valid content gives his work an immediate and enduring appeal for children.

But beauty, technical brilliance, and usefulness, although they characterize every one of his books, are not the essential ingredients of Eric Carle's books. The secret of their appeal lies deeper, in his attitude toward the young children who make up his widespread audience. It is his real concern for children, for their feelings and their interests, for their creativity and their intellectual growth that, in addition to his beautiful artwork, makes his books of such deep and lasting significance.

1. *Red Flannel Hash and Shoo-fly Pie* by Lila Perl
2. *Graphis* magazine
3. *The Secret Birthday Message* and *Watch Out! A Giant!*
4. *My Very First Library*
5. *The Honeybee and the Robber*
6. *The Very Long Train* and *The Very Long Tail*
7. *Papa, Please Get the Moon for Me* and *1, 2, 3 to the Zoo*
8. *The Grouchy Ladybug* and *The Very Hungry Caterpillar*
9. *The Very Busy Spider*
10. *Catch the Ball* and *What's for Lunch?*

Dr. Viktor Christen
ERIC CARLE: AN ARTIST FOR CHILDREN

Eric Carle has illustrated books for other writers—including Nobel laureate Isaac Bashevis Singer, Hans Baumann, and Bill Martin Jr. But it is about Eric Carle's very own books that I wish to speak, for these are the ones that have established him internationally as one of the most acclaimed author-illustrators of our time.

True Literature for the Very Young
Eric Carle's books are unmistakably his own. When Eric Carle makes a book, he not only writes and illustrates it, but he also conceives the fundamental idea of the book and all the details needed to express the idea. It is he who determines the layout, typography, and format for each of his books, and he has strong convictions about these elements.

Eric Carle makes picture books for the very young, for the not-yet reader, or those who have just begun to read. Because of the care he takes with concept and design, the youngest reader

---

Dr. Viktor Christen is Eric's long-time German editor and the former Managing Publisher of Gerstenberg Verlag, Hildesheim, Germany.

easily understands his books and loves them. He has created "toys to read" and "books to play with." Eric Carle did not invent the book-as-toy, but he has enriched this genre with many new and surprising variations, raising it to the level of world literature. In a way that is perfectly suited for his young audience, in one book he will present actions and elements that the older readers will later explore in fiction, nonfiction, play, textbook, mystery, adventure book, and so on. The toy-as-book by Eric Carle gathers all these elements between a pair of covers, and puts them right into the child's hands. His books are most like fables, parables, ballads, or sketches: each has a broad theme, follows a precise order, has educational and moral value, and meets strict literary and aesthetic demands.

The Very Hungry Caterpillar is a world best-seller for very good reasons: It contains all the elements of a typical Eric Carle book. This book can be given even to two-year-old children. They may not be able to read, but as they poke their fingers through the holes and turn the pages, they begin to understand the idea of the book. When the book is read to them, they learn counting, the days of the week, the names of foods, and so on. This is also a mysterious story

about the almost magical transformation from an inconspicuous caterpillar and stumpy cocoon to a beautiful butterfly.

The unusual shortened pages in *The Very Hungry Caterpillar*, which diminish in size as the caterpillar eats through different foods, give this book the "feel" of a toy. Many of Eric Carle's books have flaps, die-cuts, things to fold out or touch. These playful elements make a short text seem longer, and at the same time they allow the not-yet-reading child to comprehend the story. The child is not a passive listener or viewer, for with his or her own hands he or she can grasp the story's content. That is important, for it helps teach children the love of books and reading.

There is some "textbook" information about the animal heroes in Eric Carle's picture-book stories. But beyond that, the stories impart experiences involving human feelings, especially those of the child. True, *The Very Hungry Caterpillar* presents ideas about numbers, sequence, time, and biological development. But it is also a story about the transformation of an insatiable crawly insect to a beautiful butterfly rising into the heavens. It can be readily compared to Andersen's *The Ugly Duckling*. One could speak of "body and soul." In all Eric Carle's books, along with the information, there are also deeply felt human experiences and profound moral issues, and these are explored without preachy moralizing.

Like all true literature, Eric Carle's books are multilayered, and a reader can find many different levels. First there is the story—entertaining, often suspenseful and humorous. The story is often mixed with natural history infor-

mation or other educational undertones—from counting, to days of the week, to types of fruit, to phases of the moon. Eric Carle always transmits information, knowledge, reality. Never cute, never subjective, never false. However, when the child has reached his or her level and ability to understand, Eric Carle stops. One can become absorbed in his books, layer after layer, step by step. Children discover that it pays to get involved in a good book, for Eric Carle's books illuminate their world in the truest sense, as only good literature can. Those who remain involved are rewarded throughout their lives.

A Dramatic Approach to Structure
Eric Carle's books have an unmistakable type of story-stagecraft. This distinctly dramatic sense of story—the ability to structure a story as a play that unfolds before a child's eyes—is typical of his work. The way in which his material has been organized, how it is presented, how the double-spread pages follow each other, how book and toy or toy and book are joined, how text and pictures and other playful elements merge to make a whole—that is where Eric Carle shows his mastery.

Here are some of the key elements of his stage-craft: His picture book stories are sequential, based on almost archetypal models: days of the week—*The Very Hungry Caterpillar*, months—*A House For Hermit Crab*, the passage of a day, using the sun and a clock—*The Grouchy Ladybug*, colors of the rainbow—*The Mixed-Up Chameleon*. The sequential treatment always reaches a surprising peak, a *pointe*.

He often accomplishes a stunning turn of events: a double ending. These double endings may take different forms, but they are always greeted with much enthusiasm by the children. In the case of *The Very Hungry Caterpillar*, this double ending is especially extreme: on a two-page spread, the caterpillar eats the contents of a refrigerator, and the plot has reached its grotesque high point—one of the two endings. After that, a normal flow is reestablished: only a green leaf is left for the caterpillar to eat, then he disappears into a cocoon—and transforms himself into a beautiful butterfly—the second ending.

In most of his books the story—both text and graphics—end in such a manner that the child arrives at a beginning again. But these beginning-endings are never added-on features; they are always natural and logical. Psychologically, this is important because it meets a sense of play and repetition that children find so appealing. Thirty-two pages, sixteen double spreads between two covers, usually not larger than DINA 4 (approximately 8 ½" x 11") is Eric Carle's field of operation. Here he puts text and pictures into order; here he stage-manages his double spreads in order to entertain the child. The opening cover becomes the rising curtain. Die-cuts and foldouts are his props; touchable surfaces and other effects become scrims and lighting and scenery. The book becomes a stage, and the young children become actors, audience, and directors as they are pulled along with suspense.

The child is not only the audience, but the caterpillar itself, as he or she puts his or her fingers through the die-cut holes, following the adventure. The author creates between front cover and back cover a story that the child can touch and feel. Without these touchable elements the child could not travel along or be drawn into the meaning of the event. Eric Carle's play-books encourage young children to handle books, and they learn early that books are companions for life.

From the Child's View

As we hold Eric Carle's books and look at them, and as we read his personal remarks, we see the pedagogical elements in his work—how he fosters knowledge, education, and a love for reading. These motives are born of his own understanding, his own esteem and concern for the vulnerability of a child. He treats the child

With Viktor, 1971

with great care, never attempting to overtax the child's ability, recognizing the child's limits. Children should not be forced to learn; they should enjoy play. Playfully, according to their abilities and talents, children will gain knowledge. So Eric Carle knows that learning will happen when the child is ready, not when the adult decides.

Even the smallest and youngest child encompasses the whole person. The child is us, but only more unprotected, more easily hurt. The child may not be able to speak or read, but he or she already carries all human qualities and feelings, and the potential to learn, love, and suffer. This is how Eric Carle views the child. Is this the secret to his success? Perhaps. In any case, children love his books, and the books love the children right back—all over the world.

Adults may debate the quality of his work: In terms of natural science, is his caterpillar "correct"? Is the mouse behavior "logical"? Does the raised spider web "justify" the high cost of the book? Is the rooster's adventure "disappointing"? But the children's judgment is unanimous; all his books are enthusiastically accepted. We adults must be careful not to close the door to Eric Carle's books just because we may judge them from an intellectual point of view.

His success with children confirms Eric Carle. This may explain it, and it is a simple explanation: He understands children, and he can make himself understood to them. The rest is his craft.

Takeshi Matsumoto
COLORS THAT TOUCH THE HEARTS OF CHILDREN

Cities are full of colors. Posters, magazines, signs, and display windows are splashed with vibrant hues that readily attract the attention of passersby. Artists who are experienced in graphic design love to use vivid colors in their works.

Yet, no matter how hard an artist tries to combine primary and bright colors, he or she cannot always succeed in arranging them to form attractive and memorable color combinations. Even an eye-catching color scheme can fail to make a deep or lasting impression. Bright colors can be both instantly noticeable and quickly forgettable. Day after day, we are exposed to colorful but lifeless graphic matter that catches the eye merely for a second and is then tossed away. It is very rare to encounter vivid colors that possess real and memorable personality.

The first time I saw Eric Carle's works, I was surprised, as others probably have been before

Mr. Takeshi Matsumoto is the Curator and the Managing Director of the Chihiro Iwasaki Art Museum for Picture Books in Tokyo, Japan.

me, by the brightness of his colors. At the same time, I was impressed by their strong personality. Carle's picture books possess an individuality that would stand out even if they were hidden amongst hundreds of other books. His colors alone tell us a story; and it is these fascinating colors in which I am interested.

It is well known that Carle paints sheets of tissue paper, then cuts and arranges them to form a collage. The lines made with the cutting knife are much sharper and clearer than any drawn by pen or brush. Each cut of the tissue paper asserts itself. Thus, each area of color is clearly defined, giving his works keen, precise images.

Both this technique and Carle's sense of form are important characteristics of his art, but more important, I think, are the colors that he paints on the tissue paper. Looking past form, then, and considering painting in general, his various colors exist in a realm far beyond any human sense of color.

A few years ago, I visited Carle's studio. Overlooking a small Main Street in Northampton, Massachusetts, his third-floor studio was more spacious than I had expected. There were two

huge desks, one for painting tissue paper, the other for cutting or pasting the paper to make a collage. In his spare time, Carle always sits at one of these desks and devotes himself to painting tissue paper with various colors and textures. On a huge wall there were cabinets with many drawers in which the tissue paper was kept, organized according to color. These drawers can be said to be his color palette.

I asked him about the similarity between his use of color and that of the Impressionists. To this he replied, "Certainly I am inspired by some aspects of the Impressionists' work. But they are not my only influence. Have a look." He took a book of paintings and pointed to a part of a leaf, which was drawn in the seventeenth or eighteenth century. When viewed close up, the colors resembled the color and texture of his tissue paper.

Although Carle began his career as a graphic designer, his works are much closer to the humanistic world of fine arts. His wealth of knowledge of art history provides the background for his fascinating colors.

After leaving his studio, Eric Carle and I enjoyed an hour-long walk and chat. Upon reaching one house, Carle stopped in front of it and said to me, "One of my friends lives here." He walked up to a dog near the entrance. "I'd like to introduce you to my friend," he said. "He's really a nice fellow. Every day I have a chat with him," he continued with a smile. He told me that during his childhood he had adored animals.

I feel that Eric Carle left the field of graphic design and entered the world of picture books in search of warm hearts. His outstanding graphic sense and technique, and his love for all God's creatures combine to produce his distinctive style and unforgettable picture books.

Eric Carle
WHERE DO IDEAS COME FROM?
Library of Congress, Washington, D.C.

Ladies, Gentlemen, and Friends; One of the joys of an author is to receive letters from children, teachers, and parents. Some of these letters are ordinary, some funny, some precocious, some touching, most endearing. Here are some examples that I would like to share with you.

Quite a few classes do variations on *The Very Hungry Caterpillar*. I especially like this letter:

For the 1990 celebration of the International Children's Book Day, Eric Carle was invited to give a speech at a gathering of librarians and educators at the Children's Literature Center in the Library of Congress.

This is an annual event held in association with the International Board of Books for Young People (IBBY), an organization whose purpose is to further world understanding through the medium of children's books, and the Children's Literature Center in the Library of Congress, with funding from the Ezra Jack Keats Foundation, which was established by Ezra Jack Keats to encourage creativity in the arts.

A kitten grew from his mom.
On Monday he ate one mouse.
On Tuesday he ate two lollipops.
On Wednesday he ate three eggs.
On Thursday he ate one cricket, one orange, a lemon, and an apple.
On Friday the kitten felt full.
He went to the bathroom and felt much better.
The End.

Here are some others:

Elena writes: *Why do you make your animals act like people? Maybe you should write about kids.*

Brad: *I am eight years old. My dad is fifty-four years old. My mom is twenty-eight years old. How old is your wife?*

David: *I am glad that God made you. If he wouldn't have, the world wouldn't have the most famous author.*

Matthew: *Your book is like a little poem.*

Jessie: *I like how you show feelings with color.*

Lizzy: *Do you have a bodyguard?*

Chris writes: *We know that you have written a lot of books, even before we were born. They are still good, even though they are old.*

Marilyn: *I am in third grade. My teacher says all writers edit and revise their work. I find that hard to believe, so I am writing to you to find out if that's true.*

A teacher from Texas: *We read all your books we could find. My librarian accuses me of "Carleizing" my students.*

Tony: *Do you color your books or do you have an artist do that?*

Paul: *One reason I like your books is they do special things.*

Gabriel: *Do you have a wife? How old is your wife? Do you have a girlfriend?*

Rebecca: *Do you have a job?*

Adam: *I like* Do You Want to Be My Friend? *I like when the mouse asked of the animals to be his*

friend. I couldn't find any friends either when I was little.

And Sandra: *You are a good picture writer.*

But "Where do ideas come from?" is the most often asked question. Indeed, only recently a child asked, *Where do ideas come from?* Unlike the others, however, this letter writer provided me with the answer. Here it is: "Some ideas come from the *outside*, and other ideas come from your *inside*."

What is this *outside* and *inside*? Bear with me if in the pursuit of the answer to this elusive question I do not proceed in a straight line, if I jump from subject to subject.

Willem de Kooning, the eminent Expressionist painter, in whose work the critics have searched for deep meaning, simply says this about his work: "I start with a dab of red in the upper corner of the canvas, and it looks good. Then I add a dab of green to it, and it doesn't look so good. So I paint a dab of blue in the center of the canvas, and it looks good again."

Allow me then to paint my dabs of color. A dab of red here, a dab of green there. In the end these dabs of color, strung together, should form a picture. But even a finished painting remains open to interpretation.

Since this occasion has been made possible by the Ezra Jack Keats Foundation, let me begin with Ezra. I had been working in advertising as an art director for many years when, in my mid thirties, I decided that Madison Avenue was not for me. And I quit my job in order to freelance

as an illustrator and graphic designer. Portfolio under my arm, I made the rounds to advertising agencies, studios, TV stations, and publishers during the day, and worked on my assignments at night.

By the time I had done *Brown Bear, Brown Bear, What Do You See?* and began working on the first book I both wrote and illustrated, *1,2,3 to the Zoo*, a friend of mine said to me that he would like to introduce me to Ezra Jack Keats, a Caldecott Medal winner.

"Who? The what?" I asked. You see, I was still a greenhorn in the field of children's books. When the three of us met, I was struck by Ezra's gentleness, "gentlemanness," and his directness. I had just struck out on a seemingly insecure career. So far, working on *Brown Bear* and *1,2,3 to the Zoo* had been fun and fulfilling, but would this type of work pay the bills?

"Yes," Ezra reassured me. "One can make a living doing picture books." Then he showed me his studio, his books, his fan letters, and he showed me how he made his marbled papers.

He told me about contracts, royalties, and advances. But we never talked about *Where do ideas come from?*

Yet Ezra was a shiny dab of color on that canvas, and I am sure he would be pleased that his foundation has made this day possible.

But the "dabs of color that don't look so good" are part of the canvas as well!

I was born in Syracuse, New York, to German immigrant parents. I remember kindergarten there. I remember a large sun-filled room with large sheets of paper, fat brushes, and colorful paints. I remember that I went to school a happy little boy.

When I was six years old, my parents went back to Germany—where I would live for the next seventeen years. There I started school all over again. I remember a dark room with narrow windows. And I remember a cruel teacher who introduced me to a time-honored tradition: corporal punishment with a thin and relentless bamboo stick. A punishment which I have not forgotten. A punishment that stopped my enthusiasm for learning for the next ten years until I went to art school. After that painful and humiliating punishment I asked my parents: "When are we going home again?" (Home to Syracuse.) But when it became apparent that we would not return, I decided that I would become a bridge builder. I would build a bridge from Germany to America and take my beloved German grandmother by the hand across the wide ocean.

I have tried to convince myself that I should

forgive, that that punishment should not last forever. However, I cannot help, even today, to view that physical and emotional shock through the eyes of a small, innocent, six-year-old child.

Painters, musicians, and writers create mainly for themselves. First and foremost, my books and my ideas are done to please myself. Could it be that my cheerful caterpillars, ladybugs, roosters, and spiders have been created to paint over, or even scratch out, those dabs of color, which have gone wrong so long ago? Do I still seek to re-create the sun-filled room and the fat brushes? Do I still search for that kindergarten teacher in Syracuse who called in my mother to tell her that her son liked drawing pictures and that his talent should be nurtured?

Both my teacher in Syracuse and my teacher in Germany are dabs of color on that canvas. It seems, then, that ideas spring from the need to sort out, to reevaluate, to transform, and to build that bridge to one's childhood and innocence.

When, years later, Bill Martin Jr asked me to illustrate his *Brown Bear, Brown Bear, What Do You See?*, the happy days of my kindergarten came to my mind as I created those large and colorful animals for that book. A dab of color for Bill Martin Jr.

One day I was punching holes into a stack of papers, looking at the holes I thought of a bookworm; however, the bookworm would not yield to be shaped into an idea. So I turned the bookworm into a green worm. When I presented the hungry green worm to Ann Beneduce, she liked the concept but not the worm. "How about a this?" "How about a that?" we went back and

forth. "How about a caterpillar?" asked Ann. "How about a butterfly?" I shot back. And the book was finished!

This exchange between Ann and me symbolized our relationship. Never did one impose on the other. Strong convictions, yes. Power or ego struggles, never.

Many authors, half in fun, half in pain, speak of their rejection slips. I have never received an official rejection slip from Ann. Not all my ideas were that ingenious, but in our give-and-take some ideas simply and quietly were never mentioned again. Tossing an idea back and forth in this give-and-take manner might compromise or water down an idea. Somehow, we never fell into that trap. We just strengthened each other. It never mattered whether it took one, two, or three years for an idea to ripen into a finished book. There never seemed to be a rush to meet a deadline for the spring or fall list.

Today I know that Ann has that added, special gift to protect her authors from such lowly and mundane matters. A big dab of color for Ann.

Naturally, when Ann left Philomel and Patricia Gauch took over, I was concerned. Would I be able to work with this new and unknown editor? Of course, I learned to accept Pat and to work with her with confidence.

With *Animals Animals*, which was Pat's idea, she offered me an opportunity to unfold my full potential as an illustrator. Thank you, Pat.

Twenty years ago my *Pancakes, Pancakes!* was published only to go out of print within a year or two. One of my publishers recently wished to reissue this book. I decided to redo the illustrations when I realized that some of the original pictures had been damaged or lost, and that the reproduction methods have improved quite a lot since then.

As I was redoing the pictures, I was able to stand back somewhat and observe how an idea comes about and is shaped into a book. Let me try to share this process with you. The idea for *Pancakes, Pancakes!* has two "outside," or external sources.

Before I tell about the first source, let me explain that sometimes I feel like a man with one leg in the Middle Ages and one in the nuclear age. This might explain my love for Brueghel and Klee, my favorite painters: Brueghel, the painter of robust peasants, thatched roofs and country life; Klee, the seer of our times.

Pancakes, Pancakes! was for me not a nostalgic trip into the "Once Upon a Time" world. It was drawn from my own childhood experience.

My first source: Some of my summer vacations were spent in a tiny village in southern Germany untouched by modern life, a place right out of the Middle Ages. This village of perhaps a dozen farmers and their families, houses, barns, and stables, surrounded by their fields, was too poor to have its own church, but the farmers had built communally a milk house and hired a cheese maker.

In the early morning and again when the sun set, the farmers or their wives or children carried cans of lukewarm milk to the milk house. The only modern event was the weekly arrival of a large truck in a cloud of dust. The driver paid the cheese maker and left with a load of big round wheels of Swiss cheese. This was an exciting time for the children.

I stayed with my grandmother's friend, a sixty-ish-year-old unmarried woman and her old, old father, a widower in his nineties. I slept next to this ancient man, who snored dreadfully, in an enormous bed. I can still hear him get up in the middle of the night, reach for the chamber pot, and noisily pinkle into it.

I don't know whether this old man noticed me much, but I liked this gruff remnant of the Middle Ages, who, before the sun rose, would get up, throw a scythe over his shoulder, stick a whetstone into his belt, and walk to the neighboring village. There he'd lean his scythe against the church, go inside, and say his prayers. Then he went to his small field between the two villages to cut enough grass for his two cows and stuffed it into a sack, which he had brought along. They owned two cows, a pig or two, some chickens, and several hives of honeybees in their vegetable garden behind the house.

In the meantime his daughter had gone to the edge of the forest to pick wild blueberries. She'd wash them, place them neatly in a basket; then, riding on her old bicycle for an hour, she'd deliver the berries to her city client for a few *Pfennig*. When she returned, she pumped water from a well in the kitchen and made strong coffee—coffee from roasted barley—served with warm milk, dark bread, and homemade gooseberry jam. Before we ate, she dipped her fingers into a small vessel of holy water, crossed herself, and blessed us all. I remember her addressing her father in the third person. "Would father like his milk now?" for instance. This sounded very strange to me.

I was brought up a non-believing Protestant. Now here, in this one-hundred-percent-Catholic village, I experienced for the first time a rich and deeply held faith. I was told that if I didn't want to I didn't need to go to church with them. But I loved the thick-walled old church, the Latin voices rising to the vaulted ceiling, the ornate robes worn by the priest and altar boys, the intoxicating smell of incense floating among the believers, and the saints carved in wood, painted in gold and lovely hues of blue and pink and brown…looking benignly down on us.

Next door lived a rich farmer; he had about thirty cows. In the evening they were driven from their stables into a green field to feed. One of the farmer's children, a beautiful girl who was my age, perhaps ten or eleven, would guard the animals so that they wouldn't trample the adjacent fields. I joined this cowgirl to be her cowboy, and felt a strange sense of happiness. When I came back the next year to my tiny village and wanted to help with guarding the cows, my hosts told me I couldn't. After all, I was Protestant and she Catholic. How could a faith be both so inspiring and so cruel at the same time?

Source number two is also from my childhood, but from more of a "modern age" experience. During the war, when my father was away and my mother worked in a factory, she would tell me, "Make yourself a pancake when you come home from school." But first she taught me how to make one: take an egg, some milk, butter…

These two experiences shaped the *Pancakes, Pancakes!* book. Nothing of the old man, the church, my lovely cowgirl is in my book. (Perhaps these things will lend themselves for another story or two or three.) During these vacations I learned that pancakes did not come premixed in a box from shelves in a store. But most of all, I hope to have captured the essence of a bygone age, which I was lucky enough to have been part of. So the experience of the *outside* becomes tempered with one's feelings from the *inside*.

Many religions tell us about a happy afterlife in heaven or of fire and brimstone in hell. I strongly suspect that the concept of heaven and hell is based on the memory of our early childhood or perhaps on the experience of the unborn. I tend to think that most early childhood experiences are positive: the mother's love, a sense of protection and warmth.

Segovia tells us that his grandfather would sit the little boy on his knees and strum an imaginary guitar—an imaginary guitar because he was too poor to own a real one. That is when Andrés Segovia became the musical genius we know.

Henry Moore as a child applied healing salves to his mother's arthritic back. That is when Henry Moore began his beautiful sculptures.

Sendak speaks of his grandmother, who'd sit little Maurice on her lap and open and close the window shades to reveal the outside to him. In his beautiful books and now as a stage designer, the shades of his childhood have become the curtains of the theater.

Beethoven's father came home drunk, boxed little Ludwig's ears, and screamed, "Why don't you play like Mozart?" But Ludwig also had a loving grandfather. And Beethoven's music would be both defiant and full of sweetness.

Many dabs of color form that small child. Perhaps some of the dabs take a stronger hold than others.

After his dreary work as a clerk and on weekends my father would take me for long walks through the woods and fields. He would turn over a rock and show me the little creatures that scurried and slithered about. He would tell me about the ant queen who would snip off her wings after the maiden flight because once she had started a new colony, there no longer was a need for wings. He told me that trout always swim upstream. He would bend down and show me a small ball of fur with tiny bones that an owl had dropped.

He taught me that it was easy to catch a lethargic lizard in the cool morning before the warmth of the sun changed it into a swift lizard that would disappear into a crevice of a rock. He and I would mend the wing of a wounded bird.

If we did bring home a salamander or ladybug, it would be only for a short while. Soon we would release our little friends into their natural surroundings. He knew where foxes, badgers, and rabbits had built their dens. He told me why the Roman Street (*Römerstrasse*) was called Roman Street. Our region had been occupied by the Roman Legions hundreds of years ago, and under the modern pavement were still the remnants by these early road builders.

He showed me a heart with his and my mother's initials, carved many years ago into the bark of a mighty oak tree in the middle of the forest.

When I was ten years old, World War II broke out, and my father became a faceless soldier of that war that swept across Europe. And when he returned, weighing eighty pounds, a faceless survivor of that great catastrophe from a Russian POW camp, I was eighteen years old. All these years I had missed him, but when he returned, I was an art student, not much interested in the woods and fields.

Some of those dabs of paint are my father's, some mine. Together they pay homage to this gentle and interesting man, who, when he was a young boy wanted to become an artist, but whose father would not let him.

In *Gymnasium*, or high school, *Herr* Krauss taught art. As a young man he had belonged to a Socialist Youth Group, and he was a follower of the German Expressionist Movement. Socialists and Expressionism quickly fell out of favor when

Hitler came into power. Many Socialists were marched off to Dachau. The Expressionists were called "degenerate artists" and they were forbidden to paint. It was forbidden to view their paintings.

Somehow *Herr* Krauss hung on to his job as an art teacher. However, because of his youthful "sins" he was never promoted, and he was told to keep a low profile. A compromise he seemed to have accepted. I can still see *Herr* Krauss up front in the art room. He was a chain smoker and always had traces of ash all over his tweed suits. Holding up in his tobacco-stained hand last week's assignment, he'd say: "Hans Schmidt, good composition, lovely colors, beautifully drawn trees, but I can see that Carle drew this for you. An F for Hans Schmidt."

And so it would go with several more art assignments. Even though I had tried hard to develop an individual style for each of my classmates, *Herr* Krauss unmasked my crimes every time!

Remember, I hated school. I hated math and Latin. And I was a poor student. Now, Hans

Schmidt was good in math and Latin, so we simply traded our talents.

I am still ashamed to admit that I sold my talent for a bratwurst from the butcher shop of the father of my classmate, Paul. Last year, my friend, Dr. Paul Katz, and I met after many years, and we still chuckled about the bratwurst-for-art-assignment swap.

One day, *Herr* Krauss asked me to come to his house. There he showed me reproductions of the "forbidden art," done by "degenerate artists."

"I like your drawings and paintings," *Herr* Krauss told me. "I like the rough and sketchy quality of your work. However, I have instructions to teach realistic and naturalistic art and not to foster what they call sloppy work. Look at these paintings, look at their rough and sketchy quality." Then he packed his forbidden art away and told me not to tell anyone what I had seen. For having such trust in me and for opening my eyes to the beauty of the Expressionists, *Herr* Krauss deserves two dabs of color on that canvas.

Most of my books are done in collage. Collage is nothing new. I did not invent the collage; they have been done by Picasso and by nursery school children and many others in between.

In *Brown Bear, Brown Bear, What Do You See?*, my first book for children, I used plain commercially available tissue papers, which come in about forty shades. After that book, I decided to give these hues more texture and color. So I began to paint with all kinds of brushes, fingerpaint, splash and splatter onto these colored tissue papers.

Then I found out that these commercially available color-hued papers began to fade in the sun. Now I paint on plain white tissue papers. These by-me-prepared tissues become my palette.

What I am slowly discovering is that I am almost obsessed in creating richer and richer and more and more colorful colors than ever before. I suspect that I am still attempting to re-create those large colorful sheets of my kindergarten days in order to obliterate the darkness and the grays of my first grade.

If a recipe on How to Make a Picture Book were possible, it would go something like this: Take thirty-two pages (most picture books are thirty-two pages). Confine your story within these limitations. These limitations are of a technical nature. Your creative possibilities are endless. It helps to have a beginning, a middle, and an end.

Here are some basic ingredients to a few of my books: In *The Very Hungry Caterpillar*, I started with the holes—accidentally, playfully. The holes were the given. Now the caterpillar needed to be invented.

In *The Very Busy Spider*, the spider was the given. Now all I needed was the raised web.

In *The Grouchy Ladybug*, I wanted to deal with the concept of size. Now all I needed was an interesting story.

To these basic ingredients the following are added: Your love for animals, big and small.

Your appreciation for Nature.

Your father's love and his sense for passing on existing knowledge.

What you have learned from *Herr* Krauss.

You forget about your bamboo-wielding teacher (on second thought, you counteract and modify and transform that negative influence).

You entertain, teach, and challenge.

You include your likes and dislikes, your view of the world, your feelings.

And add an editor who gently prods you on.

Then like a musician, you decide on a format: Should it be a symphony, chamber music, or solo? The music should rise and fall, flow and come to an end with a crescendo or, if you feel like it, the softest bow of the violin. Then you hope for an echo. Forgive my mixed metaphors. I not only mixed dabs of paint and food but also music. But why not!

Perhaps my Uncle August had the answer to our question. My Uncle August was a Sunday painter. Sunday painters usually work as postal clerks, insurance agents, or investment bankers during the week, and paint on Sundays. My Uncle August painted on Sundays, but he didn't have a regular job during the week because on Monday, my Aunt Mina would sell his painting, and then the two would lead the high life, drinking and eating—mainly drinking—until Friday, when they would sober up. On Saturday, Uncle August got his paints, brushes, and canvas ready to paint again.

Uncle August was also a wonderful storyteller. Some weekends—happy weekends for me—I was invited to stay with Uncle August and Aunt Mina. When I arrived at their house, one of the oldest buildings in the old section of town, I'd sneak into his studio, a small unused bedroom, wait for the right moment, and say: "Uncle August, tell me a story." Peering over his glasses, he'd say, "First you have to wind up my thinking machine." And, as I had done many times before, I began to wind an imaginary lever near his temple. After a little while—all along he had made whirring noises—he shouted, "Halt! I have a story for you."

Drawing a mixed-up animal as children suggest their favorites: This is where the idea for The Mixed-Up Chameleon *came from*

I like my Uncle August's answer to where stories come from. They come from your thinking machine. All you have to do is wind it up. A dab of paint for my Uncle August, the Sunday painter.

My time is up, and I am afraid that I have been less than successful with my dabs of color and my attempt to explain where ideas come from. It seems that instead of a painting, I have produced only a small sketch. But I hope you like my sketch. Thank you.

Painting tissue papers

▶

HOW TO PREPARE COLORED TISSUE PAPERS

1.
Squeeze paint (acrylic, water, or poster paint) into a dish, add water

2.
…and stir.

HOW TO MAKE A COLLAGE ILLUSTRATION

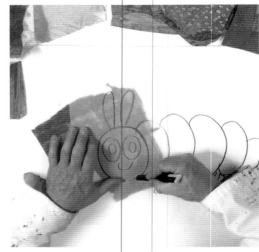

1.
Draw a caterpillar onto tracing paper or other transparent paper.

2.
Place the drawing on top of a red tissue paper and cut through both tracing and tissue papers. Be careful!

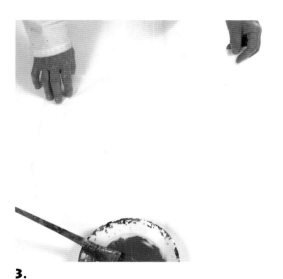

3.
Place a single sheet of tissue paper on a clean surface.

4.
Paint bold strokes onto the tissue paper. (Hint: lift up the tissue paper briefly, so it doesn't stick to the surface.) Let it dry on newspapers while working on other tissue papers.

5.
Apply a second color. Perhaps in blue wavy brushstrokes. Again: lift tissue paper and let it dry on newspapers.

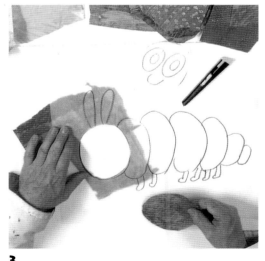

3.
You now have the face of the caterpillar.

4.
Turn the face over and apply a thin layer of glue or paste. (I use wallpaper paste.)

5.
Paste it onto a white illustration board or similar material.

HOW ERIC CARLE CREATES HIS ART
A photo essay on his technique

Eric Carle creates his artwork using a technique called collage. Even before he illustrated *Brown Bear, Brown Bear, What Do You See?*, he was using this method in his artwork for advertising illustrations (see the lobster, for example on page 35). At that time he used store-bought tissue papers which were available in some four dozen shades of color. From these tissue papers he cut or tore out shapes and pasted them down with rubber cement on illustration boards.

Later, Eric Carle started to paint on these commercially available tissue papers to add more texture; over time, however, he found that they were not colorfast and faded. He also discovered that rubber cement discolored the tissue papers and did not permanently afix them to the illustration boards.

Since the 80's Eric Carle has been using archival quality materials. He creates batches of painted tissue papers, starting out with white sheets, without thinking about how he might use a particular colored or textured tissue paper. The papers are then stored in flat files, sorted by colors, and are used as a palette for his artwork.